LOVE CHASE AT THE MOON

K. O. Nwankwo
Love Chase at the Moon

Published by Spines
ISBN: 979-8-89383-573-1

LOVE CHASE AT THE MOON

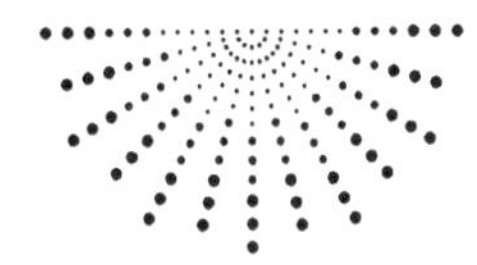

K. O. NWANKWO

DEDICATION

To the grieving hearts and love aspired minds.

INTRODUCTION

The idea to understand the dynamics of ownership and vanity often prevalent in human race is part of the subject matter, having discovered the epidemics of conflicts and war not just in Kruma but also around the world that end each historical age and restart a new cycle continuously for unending reasons.

This novel reflects the realistic framework of misdeeds and revenge which often exists when agreement or peace is breached thus portrays the humanitarian chaotic reactions over time. Mankind has proven that anger is inevitable and often superb when it meets the inconsolable minds and the reactions are always relatively similar either physically or verbally catastrophic.

In this book, each misdeed received tenfold penalty with rewards of good deeds also proportional.

The characters right here, are all chasing after something; 'love, lust, power and wealth' individually and/or collectively in unique ways repeatedly.

In this book, tribes met themselves at some point with showers of spears and arrows. This was noted as the most intense and damaging of all the tribal conflicts that occurred between the early times of civilization and the end of primitive era.

CONTENTS

1

THE QUEST TO REACH THE MOON

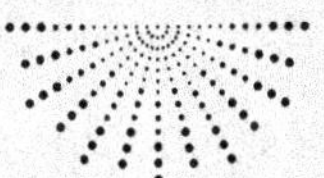

I DOUBT IF THERE IS TRUE LOVE WITHOUT WISHES AND FANTASIES

A chase at the moon could be the best love; I imagined how possible it could be to reach the moon with the man I loved so much for just no other purpose than love chasing around the moon's surface.

Deep into such an era when morality, sincerity and fidelity are bound in the hearts of ladies came his proposal for a relationship. In such a tail end of the primitive era and early time of civilization in this part of Africa, when love is prophesied to a lady, fantasies are quickly built as reality. I assured myself that the moon is the only place I have been too optimistic to reach with my soul mate (Prince Mark Morris), either by the use of magic or by science. Through this thought and imagination, it dawned on me that my quest could help our union embed historical treasures beneath the sands of the moon, which, probably in the future, when discovered by scientists, will feature a collection of high-quality ancient materials just like modern archaeologists have unearthed in different parts of the world as old human left over.

So slowly, like a medication, my love for him began to sink deeper and deeper into my soul. A week without him was in shamble. My Love mission was to enlighten people on the impressive and extreme love history that can retouch their minds, as it occurred to me that almost all humans experience the magnetic force of love at some point in life, although in different, unique ways. "We could find soft sands at the moon's surface to flourish our love chase," I said to myself. I doubt if there is true love without wishes and fantasies.

Only if we are satisfied with what this event has achieved will we forever shine fame and glory in the history log. "There are circles within circles up there in the sky that fool my mind, and I may never truly know what it holds for ages to come without being there myself," I recounted as I steadily stared at the moon.

Julia, a close friend of mine who was beaten by my aspiration to get to the moon, said, "You must be a moron to pick up the moon among all the places on earth to flourish your love when you have never even been to all the continents in the world, and here you are talking about taking up one of the best places in the sky without considering the magnificent height, but then as the stone falls the deepest, humiliation and blame will be all yours."

For such a young man like the Prince, who I loved so well, I thought of a lot of things we could do on the moon. These thoughts aren't far from bike tours and other unimaginable cruising mechanisms. But that thought suddenly came to a halt, having remembered there wouldn't be any need for that as we would be floating. I think floating will be a better cruising mechanism, after all, I told myself, as his voice re-echoed in my mind saying:

> "Whisper To My Ears
> A Whisper Of Love and Laughter
> Let Me Believe In your Imaginary
> Impossibilities
> But Then, Only If you Will Breath
> Me As your Air
> Together We Shall Open Forbidden
> Doors"

But one thing got me worried, and that is food. How do I fix our food on a planet I have never been to or seen? I can't cook there, considering the oxygen deficiency, but even if there is, there won't be a source of ignition or an element of water that could be sufficient.

Night after night of pounding over my love expedition to the moon, Julia came around. She is one good friend of mine who can't stop being hostile. She took time to write a letter and drop it for me along with the caption, "Before you venture into a planet other than the earth, carefully read my advice."

Towards the last five lines of her note, she said, "If after reading this letter you are brave enough to open your door at dead night and walk up to the end of the dark road alone, then the sky will be your achievement as you have always wanted, for the adventure you dream of, requires braveness but if you couldn't walk through the dark road then I will say you are best at bed-dreaming and henceforth you will cease bringing up your moon love topic ever again.

In all honesty, I was highly disturbed after reading her discouraging letter. Countless times, I have paused the letter for its terrifying feelings to double-check the enclosure of my windows and doors. At one point, it occurred to me that I was closing the doors rather than opening them as she had challenged me. I was beginning to think I was not truthful about my quest to reach the moon with my dearest lover (Prince Mark Morris).

I didn't find that very letter by Julia entirely odd, having realized it put me in between the balance of choice of continuity and discontinuity in my quest to reach the moon for a love date. In fact, it changed my viewpoint from an easy life-viewing perspective to an authoritarian life-viewing perspective, therefore bringing the reality of the challenges I should expect, which includes the consideration for life safety, security and other necessary physiological support we may need in the mind-proposed adventure. But when I achieve this, I'm sure my love quest will gain global recognition in two significant ways: fame and possibly standing a chance of winning the best love ever.

My heart was racing through a lot of challenges lately, having more than just the thought of traveling to the moon. However, it is a sad fact that we still have naive people like some members of my family and workmates who kept casting negative aspersions over my inspiration to flourish my love at the moon the moment Julia announced it, as they believed I was insanely in love with Prince Mark Morris.

2

THE PRICELESS CASTLE'S PRINCE

THE MAN WHO STOLE MY HEART

What I never fathomed suddenly struck me in total astonishment the moment we met in an unusual, beautiful resort in the capital city. I happened to meet the Prince at an appointment recently; he held my hand and said, "I've got something to tell you." He sat down and ate quietly. Again, I observed the hurt in his eyes, although I was silent as I always do when facing his super handsome presence. He didn't know how to say it, but he eventually did. "I want a separation," he raised the topic calmly. I didn't seem to be annoyed by his statement, as I believed it was just a dream or unreal. Instead, I asked him quietly, "Why"? He avoided my question, and that made me realize it wasn't a dream; thus, I became mad at him. I threw away every single thing on that table and shouted resoundingly at him, saying, "You are not a man!!!" We suddenly became calm and didn't talk to each other.

As I was weeping, I suddenly realized he was crying as well, though he was trying to withhold his tears. Only then did it occur to me that something seemed not to be alright somewhere, but unfortunately, I couldn't place my hands on that. Since he could hardly give me a satisfactory answer, it was dawn on me that he had lost his will to something greater than him. He seemed to love me, even though he said he wanted a separation because I could see through his inner mind. With a deep sense of guilt, he drafted a note which stated that I could own one of his donkeys and some local currency and passed the note to me. I glanced at it and then tore it into pieces, knowing that I had spent six solid years of my life with him, and suddenly, it became history.

He felt sorry for my wasted years, but he seemed as confused as I was. Suddenly, he wept so seriously before me, which unveiled my early suspicion. To me, his tears were a kind of relief, knowing that a force was acting behind his decision.

I expected him to walk out on me while I sat back to grieve all by myself in that beautiful restaurant, but he didn't. Suddenly, a faint smile dashed through my face, and I became a little bit bolder about the situation. And then I lost myself in lamentation as though I was talking to an attorney for intervention:

"Price Mark Morris stole my heart for
six solid years.
A man whom I take so much pride
in his transparency and super hand-
someness,
I have thought of so many immeasur-
able beautiful moments ahead of us,
not quite far from the love chase
around the moon's surface.
Where have I not announced his name?
Not even the dead or the angels are
ignorant of us; even my birds whistle
his name.
What could have gone wrong that
prompted such a sudden meltdown of
our evergreen love? Is this really
happening to our conscious mind?
A man I can scarify my life for,
A man I can eat his feces to keep
the ship sailing.
Who is that man more outstanding than
him in my presence?
I will undoubtedly go to tell God what
happened if, eventually, I die of acute
thinking".

I stood up in braveness, although I staggered a little due to the slight emotional trauma the news had caused me, and then walked away, continuously murmuring all by myself in what I supposed was partial insanity. Surprisingly, I woke up in a hospital bed to realize that all that happened was actually the reason why I was hospitalized.

Julia said to me, "You were probably insanely drunk, and as such, *you were talking endlessly out of point.*"

My parents said the moment they gently walked into the hospital, "You virtually kissed everyone in the house, which is abnormally unacceptable."

My head of department {Dr. Bruce} said, "You were actually acting as you know yourself, but to us, you were experiencing a mental break*down probably due to lack of sleep or intense stress.*

One of my co-nurses who secretly came to clear her curiosity asked me and said, "I was wondering if you lost a baby and your mates never knew about it *because, for the past few days, you have been asking that your baby should return to you.*

At the mention of that, I blinked repeatedly as I remembered Prince Mark Morris{the man who stole my heart}. Hence, sudden sorrow and agony returned to my nerves and bloodstream. I still couldn't believe there could be a sudden end for me and him. Not even my enemies could anticipate such separation, but they talked more about seeing me going through huddles of life without his guidance. Before now, I was working towards the acquisition of eternal love with him in my mind picture without any thought of infidelity.

Although I rejected his compensation offer, looking back at it, I was able to console myself a little bit for my innocence of anything that had prompted his actions because it was apparent I was totally innocent. That placed him on self-guilt, therefore making him offer me his donkey and some cash.

Within the first two months, I was still struggling to live as everyday life as possible while I continued to search for him, although it seemed he was missing because most people I asked his way about were actually looking for him, too.

Towards the end of the second month, I went to all the local spots he had taken me to, poured out my heart-filled grievances, and thought that the fact he was missing was killing me entirely. To wipe off my tears, I stumbled into my handbag and picked up a handkerchief, which I sometimes took back from him. I could smell the fragrance of his muscles on it. I then realized that our world may be impossibly apart. For a minute, I kept sniffing his aura and then wondered what I may have done wrong to him. With his handkerchief in my hands, I felt a sense of intimacy returning to me.

I was choosing what to wear one morning. I tried on quite a few dresses but could not find a suitable one. Then I sighed, knowing that all my dresses had grown bigger. It was apparent I had grown so thin because of the emotional chaos I was in.

My story in those local spots while searching for him triggered so much pity that within a week, I received so many consolation gifts from people I never knew in multiple numbers. Among these people came a unique woman, a philanthropist and a government official who offered to help me find the missing Prince. She is Margret by name. I felt secure knowing that someone higher than me was intervening on my behalf.

On self-command, I sat myself down some-
where distinctively lonely to reflect on our
memory lane. This critical past-life examination
with the Prince, I believe, will help me figure out
if I have unknowingly sinned against his beliefs.

3

A TRACE INTO THE PAST

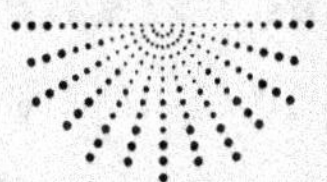

A CULTURE OF ABSOLUTE MINDFULNESS

I remember when I first began to prepare for my travel to the mysterious Kruma's ancient monarchial kingdom to meet Prince Mark Morris on a secret invitation; friends and family gave me countless suggestions that quivered my mind. But for an insane lover like me, all that was simple and natural. However, an unpredictable journey such as that with unimaginable scenery always has a fatal attraction. I was that kind of girl, on the broad way, reckless but with a keen sense of intuition and a fearless spirit.

From Zosa (my province) to Kruma on the angler's boat, the sailors were open-minded people and, of course, pitiful. After several hours, I began to sleep. Almost in the middle of the night, the dual-purpose boat gently went across the sea without encountering tempest. To realize that the Prince quietly stopped in front of my seat, bent over to offer me a cup of orange juice, wearing his usual handsome look like the dream of a prince, his face with a gracious smile; that very moment, my conscious mind woke me up. "Oh, it is just a dream of the beauty of the unpredictable journey," I said to myself.

The boat arrived at the shore of the Kruma clan at midnight. The Prince was already waiting to receive me in the light rain that was beginning to fall.

From my perspective, Kruma is a northern desolate clan based on geography. I searched in my mind for the most suitable description, and I can say it is like a land of fruitless nature. However, I became a bit curious at the Prince's reluctance to heisting up our movement to the palace. Besides, it was getting too late, but that curiosity came to a halt when he opened up and made me understand I was to be smuggled into the palace for a reason he never said. To me, I thought it could be the usual tribal or social class differences.

When this reality dawned on me that I had set feet on a strange land, my heart suddenly could not suppress the violent beat. A real panic and tension kept passing through my heart as the next few minutes were to face the unpredictable outcome and then any other kind of plot.

Notwithstanding, I found myself in Prince's chambers all alone with him as we whispered to ourselves. Even though one of his favorite securities saw him smuggle me into the palace, he reassured me he wasn't going to talk about it.

Although the next day was a bit odd watching him take away anything that mighty implicates the both of us from my handbag, such as flute, jingles and, of course, he also gave me two commandments, which are:

> "Thou shall keep silent as the dove,
> And lastly, thou shall not walk out
> of the chambers".

Nevertheless, the subsequent days were fantastic watching him treat me like a real African queen by serving me food and every other thing possible that would make my stay enjoyable. The palace walls seemed so harsh; however, it was finished in an unfashionable way. Everything about the place was archaic.

However, I had just gone to make use of the toilet when I encountered what seemed to be a drowning rat; this made me so afraid, coupled with poor illumination in that toilet. For this reason, I ran outside to check if I could find the Prince, having heard a similar voice. Although I couldn't find him, someone I supposed was the Queen (his mother) saw a little view of me. "Who is that!" she shouted and raised the alarm

for a search. Yes, I did break the last command-
ment given to me by the prince, but that was for
a reason. I was lucky he was around, and that
prevented the search from reaching his cham-
bers, although he wasn't that upset after hearing
from me.

To the people of this clan, the premarital affair is
a sin and, as such, punishable if one is found
guilty, let alone when you are caught
besmirching the sanctity of a place such as a
palace. This was when I learned one of the
reasons why the Prince smuggled me in. Perhaps
the search died ultimately because the Queen
was not sure of what she saw. This was the only
time I could remember I broke his instruction,
and that could not be enough reason to break up
our relationship after that long occurrence.

Immediately after the incident, we both secretly
and quickly left, down to a bush bar, my life for
the first time in a bush restaurant. From their
incredible eyes, I noticed that they recognized
that I was a stranger not just because of my dress
but also because I wasn't wearing any facial
tribal mark that indicated my ethnicity, as most
of them were.

Kruma is a community inhabited by rigid-minded people and everyone else who is truthful and passionate about their traditional religion. They are also a clan of people known for wearing either their sadness or happiness on their faces, as the case may be. History has it that their ancestors were ordinary humans. We were told they lived up to 120 years and practiced cultural laws worthy of emulation, a culture of absolute mindfulness.

The culture there is quite similar to a few other tribes I have heard of, especially the gender classification of welcoming a visitor or stranger- (men receive men, women receive women) and not the other way around. The people of this clan imbibe the spirit of gender inequality in the young ones through their culture and encourage every perception of patriarchy. They are also known for practicing a unique ancient dining concept among peer groups of the same gender that interlocks and leads them to discover how much more they have in common. But under the insistence and instruction of the Prince, they let me have some bush meats and undiluted fresh palm wine with him in such a discouraging lovers' district; I felt in its shadows may be hidden some biased hunger and thirst among lovers who may have been in my shoe.

Through the southern gate of the inn clan must pass through the south gate; one cannot really tell what is ancient or modern about the small district, seeing it enveloped with sun-scorched pumpkin flowers and dangling traditional gadgets, as though thousands of years of history are in it.

One significant thing I observed was the magnificent art and paintings done by old humans of Kruma, which carried so many historical and cultural symbols. Looking at the beautiful art and paintings made on the rocky walls, one may not know how to appreciate them; instead, the only thing that comes to mind is the priceless value and excitement they give the eyes. The expedition through the bush bars and stone houses was indeed a tasteful preservation of an uncertain architectural origin.

It is the most crude business district filled with seafood hanging in shops, including the world's most expensive stuck fish. Kruma is a strange place; those who buy these seafoods transport it to other African cities, I presume. I cannot help but wonder about the effectiveness of the sea trade in such old-looking stores, and the fact that every single child hangs on a tiny wooden boat hunting for seafood for sale to make a living does not make sense. What is the stress-free life that the living is supposed to enjoy in a lifetime? I asked myself. Life is too awful there. Kruma, on the other hand, has countless wealth and is the world's best natural heritage, regardless of its highly hectic nature.

So, having gone through our memories without finding out anything that could have caused the breakup, I then told myself that the sudden disappearance of the Prince was not something I could wave under the carpet. Although friends were slowly making inquiries, the search was not a type that was designed to generate a scandal considering his status.

In my life at that point, nothing else counts except finding the Prince. This further made me travel back to Kruma palace in search of him, although I came in disguise (a land dealer). While I was there, I discovered something odd from their reactions, as some of them would gently welcome me and walk away after hearing that I was the Prince's land agent. Although I sat comfortably alone in the visitor's lodge, hoping someone would lead me to him, believe me, I could see different hidden eyes spying to know my reaction from various corners. Nevertheless, I noticed the restlessness of the Prince's favorite security, who witnessed the night he smuggled me into the palace. But he could not say what was in his mind, having noticed those spying eyes towards me as well.

At some point, he stopped cross-walking and left, but after a short while, he came back and handed me a handwritten note. Immediately after he gave me that note, five members of the royal family, whom I supposed was spying on me, came out clumsily from nowhere, and one of them asked to know what the paper he gave me was all about.

I took a glance through the letter and was so upset to know that the so-called Prince's favorite security had asked me to leave in a provoking way. I looked at him like I was going to devour him. He was silent as I handed the note to the questioner and, having cleared his curiosity, gave me back the paper and asked me to leave as the security had written and probably come back the following week when the Prince would be available to attend to me.

The body language shown by all the people I met right in that palace made me believe that Prince Mark Morris was not actually missing or in fatal jeopardy. But there was something peculiar in the statement made by the security the moment I picked up my handbag, which left me confused. Although I didn't care to look at him or get clarification on that statement right inside me, I was wondering what he meant by that. He looked at me while stuffing the note inside my bag and said, "Hurry, follow the capital letters," as he pointed at the doorway.

Being a local health practitioner who can read through one's behavior, I kept pounding over that on my way home in line with his portrayed countenance towards the note he gave me. Suddenly, I was able to discover the actual meaning behind his statement, which says, "Hurry, follow the capital letters," the moment I glanced through the letter again.

From the look of things, he embedded some hidden information in capital form in the note that he gave me, which, without being told, one may overlook. His letter which states as follows:

"As the chief security guard of this

palace, I welcome you to the Kruma monarchial palace. Nevertheless, this <u>IS</u> to appeal to you to take your leave right now before you land yourself <u>IN JAIL PUNISHMENT</u> regardless of whom you represent or who you are".

Having followed the capital letters as he said, I got the following sentence: "HE IS IN JAIL PUNISHMENT." My mind was struck with shock to learn that the man I was looking for (Prince Mark Morris) was actually in jail punishment.

Upon realizing this, I quickly ran to Margret, who had offered to help me earlier. We were confused as to what could have landed a prominent prince like him in jail, and then another question was how to find out which prison he was in. After an extensive conversation, we arrived at the idea that he may not be far from one of the Kruma's regional prisons. "We must hurry to find him like the security had instructed," I frantically said. Therefore, Margret suspended her appointment tomorrow to assist me in visiting the two prisons in his region. I was confident, knowing that with her social status, we could enter the prisons without any problematic protocols.

4

THE PRINCE & THE PRISON

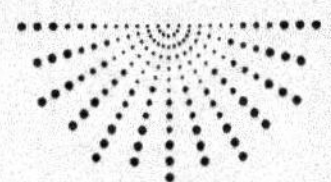

The account of his imprisonment became legendary to people when it unfolded to every ear: It is said that a particular wealth-biased dynasty (Omambala) whose source of oceanic wealth came from an ancient preserved object (a sort of magical, mystical sculpture with positive potential that one cannot really explain) which has for centuries became regional and traditional folk tales.

The late King of Kruma (the Prince's father) had traveled to meet with the Omambala dynasty to seek the dynasty's sacred power and financial boom, having been wrecked by misfortune and poverty all his life. His request was a difficult one because it forbids people from other bloodlines; however, as much as the king and his family needed their spiritual powers, they equally needed royalty as an ally. Therefore, the only way to grant the king of Kruma his wishes was through marital lock between both families and other ritual bonding.

The then monarch, on instruction by the Omambala dynasty, will perform some rituals, change the names of his children to specific lucky names, and a girl from the Omambala dynasty to be betrothed to a crown Prince of Kruma.

These tasks, they said, would bring light into the palace of the monarch, having intermingled with the supposed pure bloodline of the Omambala dynasty. The three dynasties, made up of Omambala, also agreed to help the monarch with fervent atonement for any past transgressions. Indeed, they found grace which they besought the moment he fulfilled all the instructions. Henceforth, misfortune and poverty, they said, seized, and wealth began to flow.

The Omambala dynasty is a dynasty with a superpower, and not even the monarch and his clan could overrule it. Because of this relationship, the dynasty protected the monarchial kingdom all year long, especially during the war against the Kruma people by external forces and against wild beasts that once disturbed the peace of the Kruma people.

We learned that Prince Mark Morris, since childhood, was the one betrothed to one of the most beautiful daughters from the Omambala dynasty called Zara. She was always described as Princess of the Princesses, a kind of fun way to make her feel flattered.

The agreement, they said, was to unite and marry themselves as soon as they came of age. Like the usual tradition, they were not allowed to meet each other except occasionally to prevent the sin of fornication, for their unde-filed tradition views cases of fornication with so much seriousness. They can go a long way to carry out serious case reviews as to how the act occurred. The entire audience equally had the suitor's family and the bride's family make a sacred oath that if anyone violated the sanctity of the marriage, the other party would raise an army to punish the offending party.

From the age of 21, the Prince, they said, began to withdraw from the age-long agreement. No wonder, when I met him six years ago in the local health center where I worked, he was really in a deep mind of stress and sadness for a hope-less love he had been through, he said. To keep him off the stress, I flattered him by saying, "You are such a beautiful young man." He looked at me for some seconds, smiled and said, "Beauti-ful, you said; I think the correct statement should be handsome." "Well, you are beyond that, so that's where beauty comes in," I replied. He smiled and said well, who doesn't like to be admired? You are beautiful, too". I was never interested in knowing him other than being my patient, but as time went by, he continued to resurface.

Although I am not good at reasoning, but I got a feeling that I would like him and then gradually, what I thought was a mere friendship consumed my heart following our weekly discussions and meetings. I discovered the extent of his interest in me. It was my first time to relate deeply with a man from another clan with infinite beauty. For me, I was more interested in his looks rather than the person he was. We further exchanged lots of information about our families and what we do for a living, and at that time was when I came to know him as the Prince of Kruma, a place I couldn't imagine I would visit someday, let alone frequenting the clan.

Now, going deep by what we were told by the local prison officer, the Prince blatantly refused to get married to Zara at the appointed time. Although it was not as if he was totally reckless in the marriage with Zararriage with Zara, from his account, something unfathomed did alter his love for her.

At 18 years of age, Zara was said to have suffered from a strange ailment that she battled so hard to survive for months, which left her looking so weird. Having visited her once and seen her new appearance, the Prince's notion of continuing with the marriage was killed.

To Prince Mark Morris, the aliment that left Zara looking so weird was more spiritually inflicted than being a mere natural circumstance, having known that the dynasty where she came from has a lot to do with invocation and spiritualism. Zara, too, I realized, had suffered her torment. She had poured out her heart, venting frustrations buried so deep in her, in the cause of the illness and didn't believe anything could ever have awakened them until Prince Mark Morris disappointed her.

At that moment when her story was told, the depth of her distress suddenly struck me; I intensified and began to cry. It then occurred to me that my supposed love chase around the moon's surface may be mistaken, for it is obvious that Zara has been futurizing alike. However, he made us understand he felt no satisfaction in seeing her crying relentlessly. Then I came to know why he felt pathetically guilt-ridden the day he asked me for a separation. "Wow, such a burden by a lifetime of crushing denial caused by misfortune."

"The two powerful entities reached a catastrophic agreement that they may have to live with for the rest of their lives in extreme enmity perhaps." Margret muted in an over-whelming confusion. To me, if Zara's misfortune was a mere natural circumstance, then I can say that nature played with their intelligence for having thought they had the overruling control of everything.

Despite some trepidation he stood to face in detention, we boldly hugged and reassured him of a breakthrough in no distance time. In numbers, we supported him over the devastating consequences of his imprisonment. Immediately afterward, I experienced a meltdown of ice-mounted anger I had reserved for his fatal disap-pointment towards me. All of that served no purpose anymore, and I have done nothing for the anger I felt. Although I love him so dearly, having realized his life was in danger by the dynasty, I decided to drop my anger towards him. I have learned so much from his life account; therefore, I concluded that:

"We cannot force the destiny we chose into play

when it is reluctant to favor our mind-designed desires."

It was not really hard for Margret to call for the attention of a few local politicians within and outside the region, considering her social status. The politicians whom she contacted were made to understand how uncultured it is to keep a crown Prince in jail by such an influential empire without proper judgment. These politicians, who seemed to have a good relationship with the Omambalas, were able to convince them to grant Prince Mark Morris bail on trust. At the same time, they made arrangements to decide the case traditionally as supposed.

He was bailed through the intervention and mercy of friends, but to ensure his safety, he was moved out of Kruma to Margret's house, who was comfortably staying alone in a large quarter since all other friends and I weren't staying alone. Moreover, Margret was the soul surety and promised to provide him in Kruma during the traditional hearing of the case. I shuttled from my house to Margret's house to nurse him often since he sustained minor broses from a few inmates who were probably instigated to torture him or perhaps jealous of him as a Prince.

This particular betrothment by most traditions opens one's mind to see the dangers of underage relationships, as this is a typical example of what it can lead to.

5
THE BREACH OF ETERNAL OATH

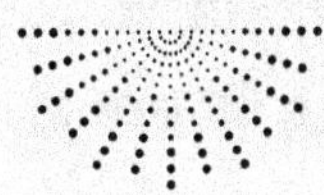

The case was shortly scheduled to be held in the empire of the Omam-balas, where the age-extended agreement was initially held in attendance of the two parties in question, three other external monarchs, the two local politicians who interceded for the Prince's release, fourteen traditional elders of mixed genders and, of course, the Prince, Margret and I, who posed as his intercessor.

That moment when everyone promptly arrived in the Empire, for a second, I felt like I had entered another world yet in Africa for its extreme beautification and glittering. It was such incredible construction that it seemed beyond the timeline it was built. It took a great deal of both taste and money to achieve. Everything about the place was immaculate. I heard their ancestors were allies of the European slave traders, and this was noted as their primary source of power and affluence, which was in line with the mystical sculpture. It was built as a defensive fortress and set in a purely strategic spot for easy slave trade.

As cross-greetings took place, wine, kola, and food were served. Here, the dynasties are noted for practicing the classical dining concept; they are set apart in groups while eating and non-family members alike. Their eating hierarchy sorts people out and also determines whether they are equal or not.

From the classical point of view, and not necessarily because of power but rather in relationship to people, a person acceptable on their table is also someone whose family might be eligible for alliance through marriage. I observed that the Kruma's monarchial household was probably afraid of food poisoning; therefore, they all politely refused to be served. The meeting shortly commenced and was chaired by the three external monarchs, which was the primary purpose for their invitation. With these three external monarchs as judges, they believed that both parties would attain fair judgment.

THE CASE WAS READ AS FOLLOWS:

"This is a case of the uprising chaos between the Kruma monarchial household and the Omambala dynasty. As history may have it, twenty-six years ago, the king of Kruma traveled miles with his family to Omambala for no other reason than to obtain fortune through the most famous

1000-year-old preserved magical sculptures of the dynasty's splendid culture.

Having faced countless untold misfortunes, the then monarch, may his soul rest in peace. He vowed before everyone to be a forever ally of the Omambala people if he successfully found spiritual power and financial revival. Upon this vow, the keepers of the sacred magical sculpture went into consultations and afterward gave the late monarch a few requirements, which included:

Ritual rites, changing the names of all his children to a specific given lucky name, and one of his kids being betrothed with any daughter within the bloodline of Omambala, which will perhaps serve as a connecting bridge to the proposed endless relationship. All the then-little girls in Omambala's family were assembled before the then-little Prince Mark Morris, the son of the late monarch, at the age of 6. He chose Zara by himself.

Further traditional rituals and rites of betrothment were carried out between the two families, and the occasion was cheerfully sealed by ensuring that both kids ate from a plate as part of the bonding, ritual and oath. Henceforward, she was forbidden from getting married to any other man as culture demands. The monarch indeed ceased to experience misfortune; instead, a financial boom was the case. As they enjoyed their newly found grace, Omambalas protected and watched over them through fervent atonement, as well as waging wars against invading forces and wild beasts disturbing the peace of the Kruma people.

Having exhausted an inestimable wealth in ensuring maximum protection to the kingdom of Kruma, they were disappointed by the Prince regardless of the oath's consequences of such contradiction."

The three chairing monarchs asked the two parties if any part of the account read was false, but silence engulfed the atmosphere for a moment. Then, a voice ruptured the silence; it was the Prince's mother (the queen). The atmosphere morphed from anxiety to cynical amusement. She analyzed what she witnessed about his funny behavior recently and disassociated herself from the turndown decision made by her son (Prince Mark Morris) and his siblings, who individually disassociated themselves alike.

Prince Mark Morris gave his reason, the same as what he told us while he was in custody, by accusing the entire Omambalas of having a hand in the strange ailment that befell Zara in what he supposed was spell-boomerang, as everyone knows that they deal more with invocation and spiritualism.

To the entire Omambalas, who strongly opposed Prince's claims but instead said that Zara, whose presence in the monarchial kingdom serves as a light, was struck by plenty of dark forces fighting the progress of the royal household.

Zara's mother interrupted everyone at a point and said to Prince Mark Morris specifically, "We have been thinking the whole thing over and over again and have made our choice. We all understand it was the unanticipated circumstance that ruined your love for our daughter. We can't defend ourselves. Anything we say will make our faces even uglier because the aliment left us no choice. The only choice is to accept the end as you have asked, but mark my word, if we did what you accused us of, we will never forgive ourselves and will be unable to face you again, but if we didn't, we will not forgive you until the end of time. Perhaps the age-long oath will take effect against the offending party.

Having been a witness of the disputes that went on in there, I decided to leave my love dreams in the hands of faith, but to Zara, she was not mentally prepared to watch her betrothed abandon her, let alone watch him floating around another woman's enclosure. Looking at the drama, it was undoubtedly a heavy disappointment for an average person to tolerate, considering the war times the Omambalas have waged in favor of the Kruma People, thus creating enmity with Kruma's rivals upon themselves. An old fellow who was present during the summit made a general proverbial statement saying:

"In The Gathering of the Vultures, One
Can Visually Spot King-Queen Vultures
without Been Told.
These King-Queens Go Down Too Dirty
Than Any Other, In Quest For The
Worst Fetid Carcass, And So Emerging
With Suffocating Stink.
Shortly after, it received purification
from a waterfall, restoring its rectitude
as though nothing had occurred.

Then, he proceeded to ask the entire audience and said: What is the actual vulture's character you are covering up as though you're a saint? This proverb, perhaps, was to tell each of the parties to rethink and re-examine their lives for a way forward in case any of them is actually behind the ugly development. Things took a more dramatic turn for the worst within the space of hours, so the three wise kings concluded by saying:

Is Obvious We Are Making History. However, Let's Keep The Candle Of Life Alive And Watch the Oath's Reaction"

At that summit, we saw the Prince and a few of his cousins verbally insult the dynasties, who were presumably their age-long keepers and protectors. The Prince boastfully proclaimed, "Just very soon, I will mount the throne, and as such, I am your law!" he wasn't wrong by that very statement. After all, he is the heir apparent and will soon be crowned in place of his late father, of which, by right, Zara should be the next lolo (Queen) and not someone else like me in every honesty. However, the three wise kings quickly dismissed the meeting; if not, it could have ended up tragically.

Indeed, it was an open episode of verbal abuse. It was unclear if the Prince was protecting the love he had for me or if he felt that the dynasty was a danger to his potential as a man.

The Omambala dynasties were not ready for the horror Zara's health kept bringing up, so they started making arrangements to send her to an unknown community, where she would receive a cure for her weird look.

On our way homeward, Zara's maid ran to us and squeezed a handwritten letter in Margret's hand to be given to the Prince for the last time: A letter I referred to as "the voice of anger & regrets."

6

THE VOICE OF ANGER & REGRETS

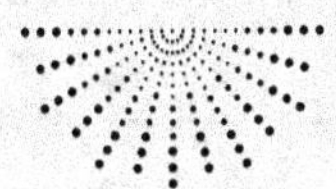

Today has been rumbling in turmoil and catastrophe over your actions, yet you turned around to point fingers as the reason for justifying what you did! Come on! That is absolutely wrong of you! Tell me this is not true! Tell me this is a joke! I have longed to be with you each minute of my life, but then, it is obvious you can't stand the test of time. How can we explain the fact that we once loved each other so dearly, yet you suddenly say you feel nothing for me? No! No! No! I can't believe this! Someone should wake me up and tell me, 'This is not happening'!

Sometimes, I get the feeling that everything will be alright, but that is only when I hear your tender voice from a distance, like a sweet melody that serenades at the window of a Princess early winter morning; sadly, these feelings melt into my stomach like ice as your voice goes farther. Slowly, just like a poison, it kills everything positive in me. Even heaven can't explain these sweet-bitter feelings to me. So deadly yet worth dying for, so crazy but so pure, trying to comprehend is even beyond my conscious mind. But in the end, I have come to understand what it feels like to love and to hate.

How could you! How could you do this to me without looking back? Even after all we have been through! How could you even think of that without thinking about how I would feel?

So this is it, right!? So this was the reason for your sudden change of attitude, right!? My heart beats violently, and my conscience completely turns blank without even an atom of silent whisper because I erroneously buried my soul in your arms over the years, and right there, it died. If I hadn't made you the keeper of my soul, it wouldn't have been difficult for me to snatch it back from you. I'm burning disastrously, and not even the police or the doctors can solve this because soul entanglement is an unbeatable case.

Nevertheless, before I turn my back on you, too, I would like to take you back to our memory lane so you can actually see what our collective race was until the evil in you brought upon us the ongoing individual race!

Once upon a time, when all things were equal and glorious, my family came up with reasonable solutions and ideas that saw you to the heights you are today! I always persuaded everyone around me for your sake when there was a need, and together, we relentlessly gave you eternal support. That was the beginning of your breakthrough. You were never the doer or the planner!

It has always been that what I accepted you disapproved of, and what I disapproved you approved of, yet nothing of such has ever been a problem in our lives because I quite understood that the issue of humanity is power and owner-ship. That was why I continually did what would please you, not because of differences in color, ethnicity, language, height, size, age or gender!

I'm so sure it has been so long since you saw those photographs on the walls of my house!? Our photographs as kids are frozen in those frames for seasons and reasons! How come you painted me ugly before everyone you and I know? Ooh, yes! I have no one else to love if I stop loving you, but how dare you proudly and arrogantly tell people that it seems I have no choice but to keep loving you forever.

You fraternized with our enemies against me, thinking I don't know!? I have always been careful not to make mistakes that will affect you, but unfortunately, everything has fallen apart just because of you! Where have I gone wrong against you!? So this is the end of our time? Having broken down my walls of defense with your power of conviction and persuasive speech!

Well, let's see if you will ever find peace! I doubt if you will! Don't ever go around telling people the ugly things in my life because you and I know that is a fallacy. The day you chose that path of separation was the day you shot at your-self—a regrettable arrow!

I cursed the day you chose to betray me! What an incredibly violent circumstance this is. You are indeed a terrible fellow! Even when my conscious mind showed me the mischievousness behind your smiles repeatedly, I boldly ignored it!

I had wished to die and get out of this miserable world to free myself from this painful situation. Still, when I realized it was a lousy wish, I begged heaven to give me a second chance at a life of breakthrough so I could prove a point to many suicidal minds out there that they could live again regardless of the situation.

While I was busy toiling and scuffling for our survival, you were busy playing around. A few times, I have asked myself, does it mean you don't care at all about life itself or that you are confident that we won't fall?? I thought you were adult enough to know what you wanted in life, but I am wrong, knowing that people still tell you what they think is best, ugly and better for you!

For a person like me whose selflessness and kindness knew no boundary, I have amply displayed my weakness without being aware of it, and I guess that idolized you before me. Even when I'm the host, the giver, the provider, the comforter, the solver, I remain the neglected, the least, the follower and the meekest!

I'm deeply frustrated again! I am facing a life-threatening disease, and I wonder if I will still rise again to wrestle with life. I have zero appetite for food, like I am facing a life-threatening disease, and I wonder if I will still rise again to wrestle with life; however, if I survive one more night, then I am sure I will live long.

Please don't talk to me after reading this! Allow me to sit in my burning heart and incubate my pains, but I tell you what, if I am choked by my grievances tonight, I will undoubtedly tell the gods all that happened, and if there is a possibility of reincarnation, I pray our paths never meet!

I traced your history back in time; you were born, hoping to come across a responsible factor for your strange way of life, but I couldn't find any. Perhaps you created the evil you have turned to be. I watched you stand still, looking on as I passed through the same huddles you masterminded, with a sad kind of smile on your lips and in your eyes! Not even to cheer me up with the enthusiasm of a loving spirit! Whether there is any logical reason behind this behavior, whether you exhibited it or not, remains an unforgettable action.

Why was everything I touched during our time prosperous, but in your case, everything you touched crashed, and everywhere you entered turned into a catastrophe? I wish I could get over this moment, but it pains me so much to realize that the more I try to forget what happened, the more it boils down my heart. And to think of the fact that this happened in a time when I had no one else other than my family to beckon for is disheartening!

For you have thrown me into a deep sea of confusion! I wish I could become a viral disease momentarily for no other reason than to munch and ravage through your whole body for an unending time for the damages you have caused me!

What have I ever done wrong to you to deserve the way you treated me? If there is a time I offended you unknowingly, you should have at least told me, and of course, you know I will apologize for this psychological torture I received from you!

What happened to our agreement!? So you knew you were going to do this all along, and you kept leading me!? How could you forget so soon about the future we planned!? What happened to the oath, the vows and promises we made to each other!? How could you suddenly throw all that to the winds!? No! You have no reason to justify what you have just done to me! I hate you! I hate you for this! In fact, I feel disgusted! I distaste a mere look at you right now!

How could you bite the fingers that fed you? How could you destroy my effort in particular? How could you have plotted against me? How come you appreciated our support and diligent work throughout your life but are not willing to love me the way I look? You forgot so quickly that life itself redesigned me the way I look presently.

We crossed you over the bridge, and all you could do was turn around and destroy that very bridge, therefore keeping many others who are to come through in perpetual drudgery just for selfish reasons best known to you!? You caused everything Because of your craftiness and covetousness.

Don't you ever come close to me should you change your mind! How many times have you run to me for help in life, and then ask yourself how many times I have run to you for help? Don't you ever tell me anything because it is all fallacy! Why should I believe you again!? Please give me a reason why I should listen to the word of your mouth on earth! Tell me one single thing you said that is true! It all lies over and over!

Is this how deceitful you are!? I thought that bringing you too close to me, even when the tradition says otherwise, would fortify me the most, and together, we can pull down strongholds, wage war against our enemies, open forbidden doors and pave a wider path for our posterity unborn. But instead, the reverse is the case! At this point, I have something to tell you: whoever amongst us dies first should not plant flowers in the other's grave! Just mark my word.

However, I'm wondering why everyone is outrageously selfish and deceitful! Why are there few good people around!? Why can't we allow the prevalence of innocence and truth to exist!? Why is our generation a generation of evil-doers and lairs!? When are we going to stop hunting each other!? What happened to our godly conscience? Where is the love that you promised!? Where is the faithfulness that you promised!?

I used to be so full of life and rich, and you knew it! I watched over you at that point! I took you and never left you behind. Now the table has turned around, and you can no longer recognize me! Is that, ooh, what a shame! You don't even know my name anymore! I hope you will be able to forgive yourself should the wind of fate turn against you someday!

I wept all day and all night, hoping you would reconsider, come to my aid, look into the past, and have mercy upon me for just a moment in a lifetime! Sometimes, I wonder what goes on in your mind! Do you really feel joy watching me in pain, watching me grind my teeth in anguish? Do you? Is this what life is all about to you?

You soon forgot how we stood by you during your hard times when no one else was there, and you soon forgot our efforts in letting your family have a royal shelter when all your extended families and friends rejected and abandoned you!

You soon forgot we fed and cared for you and your family when you could barely feed and take good care of yourselves!

You soon forgot we fasted and prayed fervently for the miracle of the financial boom you are experiencing today!

You soon forgot we were all by your side in your sick times until you regained the life that you live and enjoy today!

What more have I not done for you!? Don't I deserve to be taken good care of by you!? Don't I deserve a comfort by you!? Don't I deserve a promising future!? Don't I deserve your encouragement and protection!?

Well, you are indeed a traitor with scorching wickedness in your breath! What evil have you not done to me!? I forgave you a million times, thinking you would change, but I am wrong in my assumptions after all! If I could remember when I was sick because of the restlessness I incurred regarding you, you were not there beside me, at least to encourage me. You gave me excuses for your busy schedule as the reason for not being there for me! Didn't I forgive you?

When I was in deep trouble, I cried and called upon you! All you did was blame everyone around me. You never saved me, but I forgave you and moved on. Now tell me, who has ever spoken good of you? Who has ever mentioned your name with a smile around me? Each time your name is mentioned, ears tremble, faces frown, hearts bleed, and feelings scorch! Because your actions are often rebellious, and today, it is rebellious enough to do away with you!

Of what use have you ever been to me? Perhaps you're thinking we did all we could for you because I can't live without you. No, that's not true. We did all we could for you and your family because we see life differently. But I have come to learn the worst lessons of my life the hard way, having realized the dynamics of love, selflessness, selfishness and vanity.

Oh! You have left me with the reign of horror as I grapple for answers to many unanswered questions right before my reflection in the mirror.

But guess what? I heard my conscience say! "Hold on, my beloved, it is only a fraction of time."

Dear Prince, find the life you choose to live! But I tell you what, I will forever be better than you!"

7
JEALOUSY

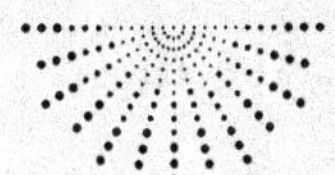

THE PRINCE WAS WOMEN'S LUSTFUL DREAMS

Having read her letter of grief to the Prince with Margret, I, on the other hand, wrote a letter to the Prince probably out of jealousy: "I think I should say something to you, for we loved each other and the love was real and thanks for the love you gave to me. Maybe this will only make me feel better after writing these words to you. The fact that we were mad at each other doesn't mean we have lost our minds and would misbehave to affect our unborn if we give this love another chance.

I couldn't imagine why you said those ridiculous words; maybe it is because we are different, or rather, we don't know how to understand each other and probably lost the faith to fix it up. You may not have understood how hard it was to study Kruma's language to get closer to you; I wouldn't have been very mad about what you said about my poor self in your dialect. It is not for my pride; it is for your misunderstanding.

I knew something had changed in your mind. It is hard work to keep a relationship like ours. Perhaps I don't see how Kruma women behave when they are in love, and maybe you don't know how my people behave when they are in love, as well as all the other differences between us. Even in your overwhelming handsomeness and presumed fragility, you are still such a man with a strong will; I am afraid I can't change you a little. Everything I did that I thought was only to show how much I love and care about you, just like a trick between lovers, ended up in unhappiness. I can't figure out what was in your mind the moment you repeatedly said it over between us, but I knew things had really changed, and it had its reason for falling apart drastically. For as long as I know, you may have had limitless thoughts and plans before saying this; maybe it is for our goodness that you choose this part.

My Prince, I'm not really angry at you. I hope you have a promising future and will meet someone worthy of your eternal love. It is just that it is really sad to let someone you really love go. What can I say at this moment? I don't know whose fault it is, but my heart is shaking.

Goodbye, my Prince. If there is a possibility of reincarnation, the love chase at the moon that I had foreseen may take place in the afterlife. The troubles merit the fact that I have met you. But if you can offer me those things you gave me before that I rejected, it will help me keep the memory of you in my mind through mere visual admiration."

* * *

As unsuccessful as it was, it seemed like it put us all back into a frame of mind that life isn't just about what it appears to be in actual reality, as it takes extreme commitment and truthfulness to keep an agreement regardless of what the future outcome will be. We all lived at some point as though we were dead inside, considering the gravity of the emotional turmoil we underwent. He was so irresistible. It wasn't just Zara and I who found ourselves falling under the spell of the prince's charisma because he also ended up engaging in sexual affairs with Margret and probably a few other ladies that circumstances brought on his path.

My suspicion became evident in the early afternoon of a particular Thursday prior to the summit between the two powerful families that Margret was getting intimate with the Prince while he was in her house. That wasn't just some sort of casual fondling, although that would be revolting enough. Margret was having intimacy with the Prince when I arrived unannounced.

In the heat of such passionate love-making, they made the fatal mistake of leaving the door unlocked. Even a fool would find that to be a bit of a no-brainer. Even at that, they seemed to forget that we were in the middle of unsolved chaos.

I wasn't sure who seduced each other, but we ended up harassing ourselves. She made me understand she didn't ask for anything in return after all. In other words, such compensating sex with my man, as she indirectly referred to it, isn't too bad to be mad at her. Indeed, the Prince was a woman's lustful dream. To think that he can have sex with another woman for whatever sentiment his reason is was totally unacceptable to me. It is pretty disturbing when you are getting along with someone you love, and someone else comes in between and interrupts. That was what I felt when Margret, whom I couldn't overrule, came in between me and him.

8

THE INVADERS

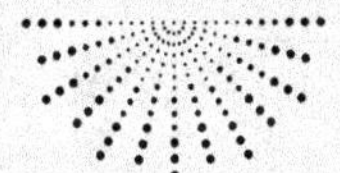

IT WAS AN ATMOSPHERE OF TERROR ON KRUMA POPULACE

Much larger invading forces arrived from four angles of the Kruma clan and struck faster than ever before. Such a fatal and ruthless attack left the entire Kruma tribe in shambles, with many treasures stolen, lives lost, and people injured in their numbers. The horror of humanity was witnessed in that attack. However, invasion was a usual circumstance considering the fact that it was an era of balance of physical power and defeat.

The monarchial household didn't escape the attack either, as the invading forces, who were often cloaked in unrecognizable animal furs, believed it had more treasure than all other houses. The entire household present on the night of the attack was severely injured, including the Queen (the Prince's mother), who was also raped multiple times.

The only exception was Prince Mark Morris, whose tentacles I believe must have signaled to him how unsafe his life was staying in the Kruma clan, knowing very well that both his immediate family and Omambala's dynasty don't see him with a welcoming smile; therefore, he stopped staying in his home town.

Why did the dynasty choose such aIf they really want to get revenge on a certain amount or type of people, the best options would have been to beat them up one by one rather than using invaders as a weapon, basically, to inflict every person that they jam with pain, injury and, of course, death? It was an atmosphere of terror in the Kruma populace; we are not talking about a few dozen over the three night's rampage of the invaders.

The community went into detail about the circumstances of Kruma's attack. The news shows that the Kruma people had placed themselves in a very vulnerable position the moment enmity kicked off between the Omambala dynasty and the monarchial household. In fact, many believed that the Omambalas may have stirred up the attack. For others, it is a fleeting moment of pain that may continually live with them. Blood ran in torrents, and drenched was all the clan.

It may interest you to know that sacred beasts in the forests of Kruma are majestic and whimsical; there is no doubt about that. They are also, however, powerful predators that can kill in an instant. These wild animals are very territorial and very aggressive, and their teeth can cause a considerable amount of damage during a frenzied attack. Such predators are drawn out by the smell of blood from massive fresh wounds, making the wounded victims a significant hazard, especially for those who ran into the forest with their bleeding wounds during the invasion.

Many octogenarians in Kruma, who had heard about the disputes earlier, warned the palace to make peace with the Omambala dynasty before the deadly occurrences. Still, the Prince, whom the situation lies in his hands, refused to give in to their advice. The Queen and the members of her household, who were also nursing their injury, were violently confronted again by a band of outlaws from her clan over the recent insecurity, as they believed that the monarchial household had something to do with the constant invasion lately. Literally, everybody was accusing everyone else of the heart-testing occurrences.

Being extremely weak in military strength, however, they were enveloped and overpowered by the mass intrusion of their people whose anger of the ceaseless attacks, sustained injury and death of their loved ones caused by the invading forces can no longer be hidden, wreaking havoc in the palace and almost caught up with the occupants of the royal household. It is obvious they have failed in their rulership; therefore, the villagers seemed to do away with their godly conscience.

The siege caused the entire royal household who were present to flee in unlinkable ways through the back exit, and each of them was destined for a different fate, including locally hired house-keepers and Prince Woloba (the third prince who is nicknamed a hunter for his obsessed hobby). Hence, the palace became a resting fortress of hopeless poor villagers who gradually, from time to time, began to besmirch the sanctity of the palace through illicit sexual exploitation amongst themselves under the umbrella of continuous protest.

The illicit sexual exploitation was not limited to young people; instead, it extended to older adults who have promiscuity running in their bloodstream. The entire episode was really the ugly side of the Act of inhumanity in expressing grievances, thus making one envisage further in an infinite thought.

9

THE CHASE DOWN THE DEEP

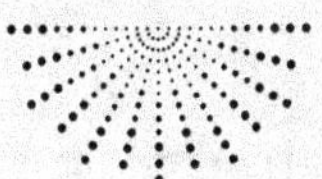

I SANK INTO AN UNKNOWN DEPTH, A NOISELESS HELL-WORTHY DEPTH THAT HAS A GARGANTUAN VACUUM

Growing up as a young man, Prince Woloba said, my life at that moment was adventurous. To conquer and explore the world around me was my supreme quest. Holidays are the most exciting moments to explore any strange or legendary forest whatsoever. In the company of my fearless dogs, we could stay away from home for days hunting and smoking bush meats as much as we could catch. Danger of any sort was the most minor thing in my mind. For someone like me who has three powerful dogs partly from the descendants of wild wolves, whose only orientation was animal hunting and nothing else, always believes in their strength; therefore, as soon as there was a siege in the palace, I opened the dogs' cage and ran away through the back gate. The dogs equally ran after me, erroneously believing it was hunting time as usual.

While I was running from the siege, my dogs suddenly went off into a speedy chase of a certain animal I didn't really see clearly in the forest of their usual chase. But from the sound and speed, one could tell that the animal in question is massive.

While I was running so fast to keep track of my dogs for my safety in the forest too, the land surface collapsed upon stepping on what I supposed were crickets' holes; thus, I sank into an unknown depth, a noiseless hell-worthy depth that had a vast vacuum right inside the unimaginable depth. Not even a hundred thousand voices could be heard from such a depth. It was echoless with unusual glittering moistures on the surface of the entire floor. I stood frightened for a long time with my two hands stretched slightly curvy like I was going to wrestle with something.

Lots of thought went through my heart as it kept beating violently like a drum beat. I refused to agree that this was my end, and then I listened to see if I could hear any sound from any creature that inhabits the ungodly underworld. However, no atom of sound was heard by me. I sniffed around a few steps away to see if I could perceive any aura of any kind of animals, humans or creatures cavorting the underworld, yet I couldn't; rather, the atmosphere smelled muddy and natural.

Interestingly, there was a little ray of light, and I could not fathom the exact source. The more I tip-toe around in curiosity with the intention to follow the lead of the light and probably escape out of the depth, the more I discover segments of empty chambers ahead of me. I felt the presence of indescribable force roaming within the vacuum. It was terrifying and mysterious to learn that a thick crowd of darkness covers my behind as I tip-toe forward in such a way that I may no longer go back to the point I started if I had wanted to, therefore keeping me either continually forward or at a place.

Having stayed for quite some hours right in that underworld, struggling for a way out without any physical torture by the unknown and equally seeing how light and darkness battle over me, I stood still. I didn't allow the grip of fear to take control, knowing that something greater than me wanted me alive.

In a brief amount of time, I tip-toed into a chamber with varieties of excellent fine sands, rolling stones and rocks; the chamber of assorted land beats in a heavy snoring sleep. Each of them was abnormally massive, as science anticipated it to be 5 million years ago.

Looking further again was a terrifying chamber with infinite chains and heaps of bones tailored down to a far end. My life, for a moment, was to be snuffed out of my body for such an extremely terrifying scene. "Without a doubt, these are certainly the monsters that chew off humans fresh here," my thought whispered frighteningly. I was determined to kill myself in the wake of any one of the monsters in question rather than watching it devour me alive. At that very suicidal thought, I realized I was not with either spears or arrows during that fatal fall. Unavoidable tears began to roll down my rough chick as I bent down and crawled almost at snail speed with utmost carefulness to bypass the mysterious monster's dean without awakening the sleeping terror.

Fortunately enough, I crawled past the domain of the heavy, sleeping, snoring monsters into another entirely different, vast chamber: an ancient-like chamber with a glittering marble throne. I took time and had a complete 360-degree view of the strange chamber and suddenly noticed a feminine being sitting and gazing at me right from the throne upon completing a clockwise view. The feminine being was elegant and adorably greenish. "Without a doubt, she could be the goddess of the underworld," I told myself. Her domain was interestingly odd to describe.

Right there, everything is sculptural, including the chairs. It was a fantastic paradise of nests of vipers, talking flowers, flying snakes and the worst of god's creations. Competitively, each of these rare creatures delivers an amazing acrobatic performance without any audience cheering them up, including fireflies bursting into the air like electrons in an easy co-existence with each other; a school of existence of several indescribable creatures and their goddess that have the power to change into whatever shape the occasion calls for. There was something admirable in what they did, and they were considered the best acrobatic performers.

Under such a spiritually charged atmosphere, all the creatures there respect and protect each other in order to rank on a scale of existence without any identifiable creature in charge of the machinery of governance.

From the look of things, they don't seem to have any lustful thoughts on each other.

From an adoring viewing moment to the sight of the petrified body of an incredible monkey-like winged creature with a dark cloud of hairs that captured my mind.

The sight of that arouses intense fear because of its unbelievable looks. The truthful side of the story is that my lips were trembling and moving, but I couldn't hear a thing. The petrified creature has been reckoned a lower-ranking god of chaos and warfare whose abode is in the dark abyss.

It was found guilty of treason and for altering the interactions between superior gods and humans. These two sins were bad enough and also threatened the balance of order between superior gods and humanity. So when some elements in its head misbehave, the superior immortal returns it to a static state and, in rare cases, into inanimate matter. When this happens, there is often a loss of an intelligible voice, which, in turn, helps to calm the problematic mentality of unnecessary chaos in its nature. But to live rightly, each creature needs to know the rules of the gods. However, to ensure that all the creatures and entities of existence have a basic understanding of the rules of gods to an acceptable degree, it is recommended that each of the creatures on assignment outside the underworld drinks from a portion called "ancient guide" as an amplifying tool in their intellect not to cross certain forbidden lines or best to say to provide an audible instructions in their minds and also for navigating the hazards in the world of man.

Each of the creatures that perform correctly will be given an eternal drink from the win pool of the superior gods before joining the heroes who have gone before. I equally saw the awful agonies other offensive creatures have to bear. Such terrible punishment was set as a warning for lower gods not to cross the line between mortals and superior gods. I also learned that the monkey-like creature is too vengeful in action with little or zero consideration for mercy and could kill merely by wing slap at or by breathing on its victims. Indeed, there was a vast historical saga about the frozen monster with many side tales, which I figured notably in that underworld. Unfortunately, the rest of the tales have not survived in my retentive memory.

In my intense confusion, the goddess of the underworld offered me something strange to drink. I was scared the drink could probably change my nature. I paused for a long while, looking at her serpent-like eyeballs, trying to figure out what could be going on right inside her mind. Still, unfortunately, I couldn't read her mind, considering her complex nature, unlike an ordinary lady who can easily read through.

Suddenly, she said in an impolite tone, "Go on! Drink it! At that moment, I realized she was running out of patience with me. I quickly drank the substance out of fear, and not quite long, she served me dinner. That, again, got me worried, knowing that my plea to return home fell on deaf ears. Right where I was sitting, I kept wondering what could humble such a powerful entity to serve me by herself. When I heard what seemed to be the crying tones of wild wolves, I asked hesitatively, "Will you throw me to the wolves?" "Ooh, yes! If it is necessary", her eyes signaled. Panic ran through my nerves with great speed.

At night, it was really freezing right in there; I was beginning to shiver when she quickly took me into an enclosure and laid me on a comfortable bed with unusual warmth. However, something still kept me bordered, knowing that she just carried me up to the bed as though I was a baby rather than letting me walk myself by her lead.

Lying on that comfortable bed of hers, my mind began to talk to me, saying: "Is it not better you take the bull by the horn and escape from here (the underworld)?" I quickly made up my mind to leave, probably at dead night, but unfortunately, when I wanted to go, I realized I could not move my legs. Perhaps she must have known I would leave at dead night and chose to cripple me with her concoction and food. No wonder she carried me up by herself into that enclosure like a baby. I was so sad I didn't realize on time that my feet had been spellbound.

"You are probably 23 years old. She asked me the moment she appeared by my bedside in the early hours of the next morning. "Yes," I replied. "I will give you the opportunity to ask me a few questions," she said to me. "Who are you?"I asked. "I am the supreme goddess of the underworld, the supreme commander of the ancient past, Mother Nature, the keeper of your ancestors," she murmured in reply.

"Where am I?"I asked. "You are in a new world; you will soon find out," she replied. Forgive me for asking, 'Are you a human or a spirit?'"I have both natures, my young friend, "she replied

"I suppose I am still alive, or am I dead?" I asked out of curiosity, hearing her refer to herself as a half-immortal being. "You're alive," she whispered gently.

"Are you actually going to kill me"? I asked. "If I were going to kill you, I would have done that long before now. You are safe with me," she replied gently.

"You stay here all by yourself?" I asked. "My unsullied worshipers have all gone to carry out their duties in the world of man. They will soon arrive," she said with a faint smile.

"Worshipers, you said? Do I believe you are God?" I asked. "God, you said, I can't take his place. He remains God, but I share the same features with him". She mumbled.

"You just said you share the same feature with God. Can you get me out of this situation (this underworld)? I really need to go back home to my family. They must be looking for me now," I asked. "I will let you go home, but not so soon," she said.

"Why won't you let me go so soon, if I may ask? Have I committed any offense? Look, it wasn't my intention to get into your domain. I'm sorry for trespassing. Please show me a gateway out of this place. Can you?, I asked. "Your presence here is part of your designed destiny; therefore, until you are familiar with the knowledge that has to do with your destiny, only then you shall return home", she replied.

"So what do you do here, and for how long have you been here?"I asked. "My work is to spice up the nature of mankind, negatively or positively as the case may be, and I have been here since the beginning of my time," she replied.

Suddenly, one of the unsullied worshipers (a masculine-looking being) she talked about arrived in her presence with two sets of hefty, blood-bathed dead creatures. She looked at him in amazement and said. "Your kill?" he looked at me for a while and answered her, "Yes, they ran into my trap." He went on dragging those dead creatures into a place I suppose could be a coven. From what I observed, he basically brings the souls of animals of all kinds across an inter-dimensional portal to feed the souls of the ancient ones.

Surprisingly as it may sound, I woke up from a coma to discover that all my encounter in the underworld was just a dream and also to find myself in what seemed to be a primitive clan of similar-looking women, notably filled with human nests in different segments built on the slopes of high hills anchored beside enormous trees and boulders that seemed to be deeply rooted into the ground and to be told by those women that I had slipped and fell off the cliff down to the foot of the mountain into their farmland while chasing after my dogs that were chasing the supposed massive animal I couldn't see.

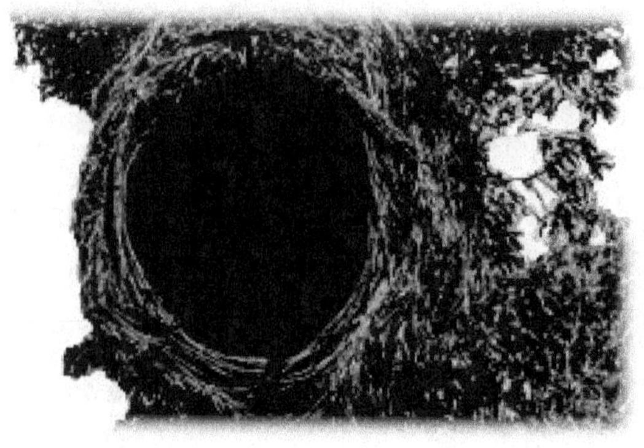

This primitive-looking tribe was more of an unusual populace of women with bountiful facial resemblance, which I suppose is an inter-play of genes caused by their devoted inter-marriage style of life between extended families and everyone else who is relatively close, hard-working and merciful. A transcendent clan in which there is neither suffering, desire, nor sense of self. They are also a clan of people known for wearing their goodness through their smiles and approach. History has it that their ancestors were fewer noblemen and many women. Indeed, it told us the men died early while the women lived up to 90 years, and hence, they accommodated inter-marital laws to meet the need for procreation.

They were considered powerful enchantresses, versatile in the arts of herbs and potions, and capable of renewing and healing any sickness. Here, young parents effortlessly imbibe the spirit of equality in their children and debunk every perception of family leadership reckoned through the male procession since the two-thirds majority are women. They are equally known for their communal dining concept, a concept of well-being, whereby most foods, especially meat meals, are eaten on fire as a consecrated meal. It is noted that certain foods are not given or eaten together with strangers. Every particular meal has a classified age or gender who prepares it, so as a matter of fact, it matters desperately who cooks the meal; therefore, when the age or gender is misplaced, it is impermissibly defiling the communal dining culture. On a large scale, the meals can also be seen as a symbol of a shared bond in bringing family members together and contributing to their spiritual and social well-being.

They continued to feed me with reviving concoctions and foods over time since I sustained multiple bone fractures that left me temporally crippled. I couldn't help but be grateful to see how the women moved me around from position to position, especially when they wanted to clean me up. Not quite long I learned that the tribe's deadly trap killed my two dogs. To think of the fact that the two sets of hefty blood-bathed dead creatures, the insulin worshiper, came in within the supposed underworld where the bodies of my dead dogs are disheartening. In fact, it dawned on me that even as I was in a coma, I had some knowledge of what was happening around me, through in a different view.

Among these similar-looking women was a light-skinned, innocent, gorgeous, gorgeous-looking young girl who refused to have her face pierced as their custom demanded. A girl whose lineage and ancestors I learned belong to formidable sorceresses. History has it that they were the institutors of the ancient knights (the moderators of customs and tradition in this clan). She was probably ignored because of the unquestionable powers in her family's posses-sion; otherwise, she would have been forcefully subjected to the usual tribal mark popularly known as the all-for-no-mercy piercing process like everyone else.

That drew my attention to the fact that there are people laws aren't meant for. She often comes around to watch me from a little distance away without saying a word. She is an exceedingly beautiful maiden sought by an army of suitors. She could not help being sorrowful at finding me already so impatient to begin my adventures back to my clan. I saw in her eyes a light that led me to greatness. Often, I visually take a tour of the most excellent curves on her body without leaving any suspicion of lust. Indeed, she captured my mind, and I was able to recover fast, hearing what seemed to be her constant whistle echoing melodiously in the air.

The people of this primitive clan have mastered and maintained the ancient art of calling their flocks home with mouth whistle or rather high-pitched melody that echoes very far across farm-lands, hills and valleys. In such depths of harmattan as it is now, food is desperately hard to find. The head of the herds leads them to the edge of their territory. In these mountains, any food found by these flocks is precious. There was hardly enough to sustain the entire flock, yet they grazed it peaceably.

10

THE QUEEN & THE DWARVES

A CULTURE OF MOMENTARY WAYWARDNESS

According to history and the timeline of events, the Queen stumbled out of the forest into a strange clan after a long race, having been chased away by the angry co-villagers (her subjects). This extraordinary clan is said to be ruled and inhabited by the most famous dwarves and everyone else who is short, ugly and good. They are also a clan of people known for wearing their desires right in their eyes and body. History has it that their ancestors were untraceable strangers, and nothing is known about them, thus leaving a vast gap worthy of investigation.

It is often described as an ecologically assorted natural reserve in the northwest, with a varied landscape composed of moors and valleys, many of which are covered with age-long oak trees; the Dwarves clan is a popular destination for hunting adventures.

In fact, many cast their traps into the thick forest, hoping to catch one of the abundant animals that move across its physical geography. Among other ethnic groups slightly far within, the dwarf's forest is one of the safest forests so far, with less harmful land beasts. It features a fabulous variety of scenery and is deservedly popular with day travelers and night hunters across its land space.

It is interesting to note that the customs there are very different from those of the rest of the world, especially their half-nude way of dressing and their unique way of welcoming a stranger or visitor with wine made of animal blood and toxic flavor.

It is pretty strange to see an entire community filled with a variety of ugly and beautiful dwarves with irresistible curvatures, especially their ladies. History has it that these famous dwarves' community was established by early men as a human dump site aimed at keeping dwarves and people with deformities from birth only as soon as they are raised. They were believed to have reincarnated to pay the price for their past life transgressions and, therefore, were inflicted with bodily curses by nature itself. For this reason, they were further pushed into the forest to settle. It is best described as a land of stunning ramshackle houses and ancient remnants, and it is a place of complex culture.

The dwarves are the centerpiece of curious travelers who pass through their community. Since one can hardly say who is old among the dwarves, visitors often say they embody a youthful, staunch look. History has it that they have never been invaded by any invading forces, probably because they were seen as cursed people or because they were known for keeping fortified shrines.

Notwithstanding, the Queen of Kruma seized the opportunity to pray for the presence of the gods of the dwarves, thus calling upon the impeccable gods of war and retaliation, the ancient powers of rulers of the deep, the supreme commander, as well as the guardians of the peripheries of dark forces to bestow upon her extraordinary powers of eternal sorcery and to inspire her to endure the reign of her emotional agony.

Nevertheless, in the center of the community is a vast square naturally surrounded by trees. Travelers often put up their tents and pass a night if they are tired or probably when they encounter darkness and can no longer continue their journey. The dwarves utilized such stopovers well, and they were glad to interact with different tribes passing through their clan. These dwarves often offer drinking water, the usual sweet wine made of animal blood and toxic flavor and also keep company with the travelers, whom, in some cases, dish out gifts and cowries (money) in appreciation for their generosity, thereby enriching themselves individually having known that the more travelers they host, the more wealthy or materialistic they become.

It is remarkable that such a heart-melting favor offered by the dwarves encompasses the exciting world of total dedication and also creates admirable expression. Their service often bursts into the minds of their visitors in absolute happiness, thus triggering sexual intercourse as a way of reciprocating their appreciation towards these dwarves as they pass the night in what seemed to be a fire campground.

Most visitors derive much pleasure by voluntarily stopping over in this clan for just that purpose and to watch the smooth mechanism of their hips and short legs as they move.

Today, they have successfully survived and established the dwarf community. Indeed, hope, they said, can grow from tragedy. Irrespective of many ramshackle houses bound within the remnants of the ancient dwarves forest and several other smaller settlements scattered around, the dwarves share limitless happiness and peaceful coexistence among one another, which is supposed to have been achieved through the practice of illimitable inter-racial intercourse with strangers.

So primitive as their beliefs seem, peaceful co-existence has only one way to be achieved, and that is by sexual gratification, without which nothing else can maintain ultimate peace: a culture of momentary waywardness.

The queen of Kruma is obviously the first tall lady who has officially come to live with them, either temporally or permanently, as the case may be. She found refuge and allies with the dwarves (the ruling family, of course). The dwarves are well known to be polygamous; therefore, it could be a reason why she was quickly accepted into the royal household there, but soon, the wives of the ruler became increas-ingly suspicious and jealous of her presence and her charming charisma that left every dwarf male within, in mind fantasy. In her relentless thought towards coming up with a good idea to save her clan and return home, she began to notice strange feelings over herself.

She observed she was pregnant, although she strongly disbelieved that someone of her age could conceive. As days ran to weeks and weeks ran to months, it became apparent doubtless that she was pregnant with a baby. Many of them within the dwarf community strongly rumored and believed their ruler must have gotten her pregnant. To the queen, she knew that her pregnancy was a result of the multiple rapes carried against her during the invasion of her clan. She was disturbed knowing the fact that a royal widow like her would soon give birth to a bastard, but on the other hand, she thanked the gods for bringing her to such a strange clan where she could personally cover the shame even after giving birth to her bastard.

11

THE MULTICULTURAL SQUARE

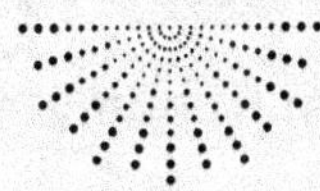

The varieties of intercultural dressing each of the many visitors portrays right there at the dwarves 'village square offer a uniquely different view of that square. With time, the vast square turned from its original purpose to a scenic site or, best to say, the most important ceremonial center and then again to a multicultural market square as it gives the opportunity for barter trading as well as cash trading.

Since the square became famous, such an open field also became a place of excellence. Each clan and its people often come to display their cultural variations, heritage and pride. It is usually a colorful traditional day with each of these participants chanting their own dialect as they sing and dance one tribe at a time. It was never a ritualistic occasion but rather a sport–like the occasion of merry and happiness.

Interestingly, each of these tribes has something they were called and known for. For instance, The people of feathers are known for using all kinds of assorted birds' feathers in making their clothes. This very tribe is the tribe of the unusual populace of women with bountiful facial resemblance. When they come out to display their colorful cultural heritage through dancing, people pay unique attention just because of these feathers and perhaps their identical looks caused by their devoted intermarriage style of life between extended families. One can even hear people calling out names of birds whose feathers were on display. An army of suitors often seeks this identical clan of people, and that's the pride accompanying such cultural display.

The people of nature (the dwarves) are known for their nudity. They were so backward and natural that they took great confidence wearing their skin basically to draw attention to themselves and to their clan, which they have successfully achieved, although, with many paintings and tattoos done on their bodies, one could hardly know they were naked and that's the point of interest too. The paintings on their bodies were not just done for no reason; they represent so many beliefs, circumstances, birth, rebirth, symbols, age and time. People find it so interesting trying to figure out the meaning of those marks and paintings so as to know the depth of one's existence, while some other's interests were on beauty, perfection and curvatures.

The people of animal skin (giant tribe), who are often cloaked in animal furs, are known for their might in pulling down weak and robust beasts. Their cultural heritage is renowned for hunting for skulls and skins. This tribe believes so much in its strength and power. During this display, their pride is often noticed. They were men and women on assorted animal skins. People find them unique, especially when they spot skins like lions, tigers, leopards or rare animal skins.

People of leaves are known for using leaves in making their outfits. They believe so much in leaves, and this enables them to master the art of entanglement and twisting, be it dry or fresh leaves. Although people tend to laugh so loud as they see leaves move, bend or twist, they are less attractive.

Last but not least are the people of fabrics and textiles (Kruma and its ally-the Omabala). The big and smallish clans often fraternize together during this cultural display. They were known for being spectacular, fantastic, and far more forward than any other tribe so far. Hand-waving clothes in such an undeveloped time was relatively new. This tribe is often the centerpiece of attention during this annual occasion. The rest of the tribe usually wants to see the type of clothes they will display.

The secret of the knowledge of their fashion antiques was often rumored around the occasion ground, which they said lies on ome-efe. A hand-weaving tailor who was so famous for making clothes for his people alone. Many said he takes instruction from a strange creature who has mastered the art of ancient fashion. Although no one has seen the beast, people believe it dwells in a bullish sack right in his corner. The bullish sack is said to often rumble from time to time, indicating the presence of a creature in it. Others believe there was no creature in the sack—instead, his tailoring materials and possibly some rodents or rats that may have taken refuge in it.

The later account was discredited for some reasons. Ome-efe, they said, was a complete man until he met the creature in the forest known as the "talking bush." The beast, they said, made him a promise and, after that, sealed his lips to talk less or nothing about it. Ome-efe indeed became the village's glory.

The forest (talking bush) is a bush of magic and mysticism. It was also a place where supernatural forces battled for supremacy. Most miraculous encounters people had right after visiting the forest were in their favor, except for a few who died trying. When such circumstances of untimely death occur, people are reminded about the variation in luck, success, and destiny.

The talking bush, they said, is a place where people with unique gifts visit to seek divine help in developing their God-given talent. However, one must be clean (sin-free) before stepping into the forest, or else the tragedy of one's untimely death is bound to happen. We were told you don't just step into the forest to make a lamented request and leave; rather, one who is seeking a divine encounter must be prepared to live there for as long as it takes to meet the right spirit carrying the blessings you pray, only then you can be successful.

Nevertheless, it was called the "talking bush" because of the mumbling voices often heard by visitors and farmers who use that route to reach their farms. According to history, these mumbling voices were feral and not entirely human, although, in such animalistic speech, something could be understood. However, it is sometimes incomprehensive or altogether esoteric.

Although it was widely referred to as the talking bush, few other villages call it the forest of the First Men because of its historical attribution to the First Men. These people, however, believe that the spiritual activeness in that forest is a replay of energy from their past existence. The information in records also said strange-looking beings were also sighted, and they did not look anything close to humans, let alone first men. For this reason, the forces remained an unsolved historical mystery; therefore, each clan had its own beliefs to their own believe.

Oh yes! Ome-efe had visited the forest of the first men, or rather, the talking bush, before what happened to his lips, but no one could rightly tell the actual account that led to his success in hand tailoring since he was dumb.

From historical reality, the forest had received quite a considerable number of people, of which Ome-efe was a few of the famous visitors. But that's by the way. Having carefully narrated her (queen) ordeal to the dwarf ruler, he quickly sent his spies to find out where the invading forces emerged from. They soon returned after days with valuable surveillance.

12

QUEEN'S JOURNEY TO THE GIANT TRIBE

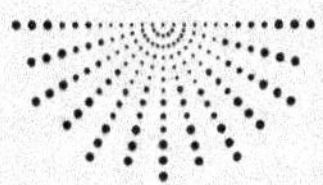

A NASTY OFFER WHICH WAS TO PERMIT THE BOY LIFT UP HER GOWN AND SEE WHAT IS HIDDEN IN-BETWEEN HER LEGS'

oon enough, the queen of Kruma set on a journey with a donkey to the land of her invaders, torturers, enemies and killers, aiming to find a long-lasting solution to the age prolonged torture carried out against Kruma people, even if it requires scarifying her own life. The recent attack on her tribe was said to be the longest, darkest, and bloodiest in history, lasting for days, followed by a long period of agony, mourning, severe hunger and hardship. Although she dressed as a farmer to conceal her true identity for safety reasons, yet one can still see a trace of royalty while looking at her.

It took quite a long time to arrive in that clan (the clan of her invaders), a clan ruled and inhabited by the giant, pot-belly, carnivorous-looking men and women and everyone else who is vast, monstrous and evil. They are also a clan of people known for wearing their wickedness on their faces and characters. History has it that their ancestors were the earth's first humans who migrated from the legendary forest of the first men. Although history didn't tell us the length of time they lived, we were told they engaged in so many physical demonstrations, which was quite incredible.

The clan is often rumored to be the deadliest of all clans for the continued disappearance of foot travelers and visitors who mistakenly stumbled into the village. Life would have been hard for the giants if not that they depended mainly on oppressing and invading so many tribes for their survival. People who know this deadly clan in this part of Africa do not wish to visit them from year to year.

However, it is sometimes difficult to balance their needs, knowing very well that no one wants anything to do with them. As such, the giants take up invasion and raiding in full range as though it is a legal occupation, conquering many tribes and refusing to fall prey. However, the reverse was the case when the giants encountered the charming queen of Kruma.

Where she stood on her donkey gazing across the stream of the treacherous town, she was captured by five boundary watchers. They were actually setting massive traps in a horizontal dimension aimed towards protecting their boundaries from any form of invasion by their rivals. As soon as they tailored the trap down the valley, they rough-handedly brought her to the presence of their King. He was such a brutal-looking fellow, too. Looking at him, she remembered the night she was mercilessly raped: a night of communal terror and brutality, a night she thought was the end of their lives. It is obvious he was the one responsible for her pregnancy and perceptibly the manipulative mastermind behind the series of raiding and killings, if not for anything, at least for the same remarkable scar on his face. That moment, when she looked into his eyes, she saw a man with no heart, and she also knew his lust for her had returned. He is known for his intense desire for beautiful women like the Queen of Kruma; He is a man who craves the lust to succeed in all his evil intentions.

Ironically, the Queen of Kruma isn't a giant as she felt while with the dwarfs. The giant monstrous King, who seemed to recognize her too, waved at his subjects to leave and then again raped her without speaking a word, not minding she was pregnant. As he sat at a corner drinking a jug of wine and staring at the queen of Kruma, who he had just raped, she made him understand that she was pregnant for him and, as such, she had come to deliver the baby for him.

Although he still didn't say a word, she believes he heard her. She also pleaded with him to handle her gently, and she will be glad to share her body with him at any time he demands.

At the mention of that, his countenance signaled a welcome to the queen. To gain his trust and possibly take control of him, she became immeasurably obedient and respectful and constantly showering praises at him. She aimed at making him feel majestic and flattered even though he seemed unemotional, but his heart smiles often, she felt. It is so weird to know that the customs there are very different from the rest of the world, especially their harassment and unwelcome looks given towards strangers or visitors. Here, parents imbibe the spirit of chaos, tribal dominance, and hostility in their children and debunk every perception of uprightness. They walk by that footstep: a culture of theft, raiding and brutality.

Indeed, getting lost is realistic unless you have an experienced guide. Ancient rumors speculate that the swirling sea breezes that once passed through the giant tribe were full of grit, and thus, they sculptured those treacherous rocks. The treacherously mountainous kingdom is the most prosperous land in the world due to the overwhelming numbers of stolen treasures, ornaments, precious stones, diamonds, gold and silvers from weaker, far and near tribes. It is best described as a breeding ground of evil, a land of stunning mud castles and rigid culture. When one talks about a place with the best mud castles and fortresses, the giants have a significant taste for it.

Haven adjusted to her new world carefully; the queen, hence, voluntarily built high sexual pleasure with him, thereby making him believe he was the man of her desire. From his body language, he was so delighted to have the queen in his sinful arms at all times, ravaging through her irresistible beauty.

Bearing in mind how responsive he eventually becomes to the queen's quests, ideas, hates and likes, one would bet he must have been wishing for a lifetime of love chase or lust chase with the queen in god knows the planet of his fantasy just like every one of us had hoped for a love chase at the moon with our own desired lover. She did experience one of the most beautiful sensational feelings considering his strength in bed, even though her submission was for a hidden purpose. Such long sexual moments were more fulfilling in a physical sense if she was indeed in love with him, she revealed.

The ruler, who is said to have strangled his wives at different points in his life, could not harm the queen, possibly because of her charming look, dove-like character and obedience. As they stayed together often, they eventually began to talk. The queen, on the other hand, began to intercede for the safety of the Kruma people. What was surprising is that his people obeyed and stood by him no matter how many crimes they masterminded together. Also, considering the fact that civilization was young at that time and hadn't grown past primitive dealings, no one could put a quick end to the situation. For six months, no one has heard or seen the queen of Kruma and her royal household.

Surprisingly, Prince Mark Morris knocked and walked into my apartment. I felt as if I was suffocating in joy, but then again, I thought I should jump up, out of overwhelmed surprise, for returning to me at last after reading my letter.

Heaven must be praised! I shouted. He kept smiling and looking at me, and then I asked him and said "so all these, while you have been fighting off Zara, was just for me? He replied me and said "not just that, but I have equally come to fulfill your dream –the love chase at the moon surface." "Really," I said in amazement; he continued and said, "It will surprise you to know that I have made all the necessary arrangements for the space travel; we must go now."

At the mention of that, I was awakened by a heavy knock; I opened my eyes to realize it was a dream. I reached the door angrily, and surprisingly, it was Margret. We gazed at each other and realized that both of us were wearing sad faces, and that made her ask me and say, "You must have heard the news."? "What news?" I asked. "About the prince," she replied. "I have never heard from him for months now. In fact, I just dreamt of him just now, and that made me sad when I realized it was a dream", I said. "Well,

I have come to tell you that Prince Mark Morris is dead." I paused in shock, and she continued. "On his way to his clan upon hearing that the palace is under siege by the villagers, the boat in which he was capsized, and he died along with the sailor and an unidentified old fellow on board." I was in open-mouthed astonishment, and suddenly, my body began to shiver in great force, and I passed out.

Unfortunately, everyone involved in the so-called love triangle with him eventually spent a vain moment. To the traditionalists, the breach of the oath of betrothment must have been responsible for snuffing life out of the prince; therefore, this proved the innocence of the dynasty as he accused them of being responsible for Zara's misfortune.

, can sincerely admit we were all in search of one thing – a golden love or a love chase, best to say, Yes I can sincerely admit we were all in search of one thing – a golden love or a love chase best to say, but when I saw this reality clearly, such a life of love pursuit felt a little lighter. I felt like I had gone through the shadows of love for eternity to achieve nothing. To live with oneself in fullness without him seemed impossible; therefore, I often go up to the mountains most evenings to have a glimpse of the moon to rekindle my hope and possibly lament my wishes to nature.

There was this feeling that usually accompanies me home each time I visit the mountain. I could feel as though I'm the source of love, the giver, the gifted, the lover, the host, all at once. These feelings filled my emptiness as I speechlessly walked in an empty mind, waiting for life itself to teach me how to live alone again. I have to be patient and watch these feelings blossom within me at the sight of the full moon. I can't count how many magnificently beautiful mons I have ever witnessed. The east and west must be the face of nature to have chosen the rise and fall of the moon in those directions. If not the face of nature, then it must be the most beautiful side of nature.

"The east and west must be the face of nature to have chosen the rise and fall of the moon in those directions. If not the face of nature, then it must be the most beautiful side of nature".

To the queen, having stayed a bit long in the giant tribe, she decided to know if she had gained the King's heart. Her idea was to tell him that she wanted to visit her clan. If he allows her to go quickly, it means he has no good use for her, but if he refuses, it means her presence means a lot. With this idea, she will know the next level of manipulation she could take.

Eventually, when he was told she wanted to go, his countenances changed, and within a little while, he surrounded his home with guards. She gave a faint smile, knowing that the monstrous king had given in to love or lust. The queen of Kruma began to use her pregnancy as an excuse for walkout excise. This permits her to walk around the village with a guard, aimed to survey the entire clan and its approximated population visually. This, she believes, will enable her to know where their strength lies.

While she was there (the giant tribe), she made some friends, basically teenagers far below her age, so as to play on their intelligence easily through these teenagers; she also learned that the Omambalas never instigated the recent attacks on the Kruma people. The giant tribe is said to have earlier planted their indigenes in different communities who live and work as farmers, fishermen or traders with the sole aim of spying on the targeted communities where they live.

As we know, the Omambala dynasty had modern weapons and wicked forces that could counter any force within the region. Therefore, any community allied with the Omambalas was regarded as untouchable. Soon, the giant tribe learned from their spy about the disputes going on between the royal household and the Omambalas. Thus, the giants decided to strike Kruma, knowing fully well they would not be protected at the peak of their problems with the dynasty.

They were not wrong in their calculations after all. To the queen, it takes nothing more than a slice of smoked fish to get an untold secret out from her little friends. But not quite long, she also realized it takes more than what she thought to get more dreadful information from one of the teens.

Thus, the giants decided to strike Kruma, knowing full well they would make him a nasty offer, which he couldn't refuse; he broke the oath of secrecy.

The house where only men enter, he revealed, is said to be the house of captives of war who were mostly gorgeous tall women, referred to as baby-making captives. To ensure loyalty from another clan, the giants invaded, and the heirs and daughters of the local rulers were taken and kept there as prisoners in their community. In this place, they forced the ladies to bend over and grab the rough bumps of rocks situated in there while the giants lavishly toil and jerked with their bodies until they got themselves entirely out of breath, without being able to get the satisfaction they needed. Right there, it occurred to her that the giant tribe isn't just after treasures but also taking in hostages; such a unique secret that keeps the mind racing through lots of thoughts.

Not long after revealing the vital secret to the Queen, the teenage boy died drowned in shallow water. Indeed, the oath of secrecy was valid.

While the Queen lived together with the monstrous King, it was the first time he heard his real name spoken in his whole life as a King by the Queen of Kruma, whom he believed must have gotten his name from her fellow women. At the mention of his name with her gracious smile, it got him a little overjoyed.

It was noted that his first murder happened in his late 20s in his quest to become a "mantle holder."He was said to have brutally murdered his uncle, who was the king at that time. In contrast, another contrary account said he accidentally begot a daughter with his blood sister 'Ure' in a night of blind lust (a night of heavily drunken state) and then killed his uncle, who was the then king, to prevent and conceal any form of punishment that would have been unleashed on him. Such a heart-sweetening iniquity that often leaves the mind regrettably eyes open moments after commitment whispered the old humble, looking lady who sounded too bitter towards their monstrous King while massaging the queen who was going to give birth in a few days with hot water.

'Such a heart-sweetening iniquity that often leaves the mind regrettably eyes open moments after commitment'

Shortly afterward, he became the most feared man, and she further revealed that he was conferred with the ruling power as the king. He then seized the opportunity to act on the dark side of the thoughts that had long been growing in his mind (the idea of raiding and brutality). He was described as neurotic and believed that destructive demons had long possessed him.

It is believed that the soul of man rejoices at some memorable moments; therefore, the monstrous-looking King was experiencing the said soul's happiness the moment the queen of Kruma gave birth to his baby. Not just a baby, but a valuable one (an heir apparent to his throne). For this reason, he ordered for a tank of local sweet wine and invited his sixty undefeated giant carnivorous-looking forces of mixed genders to wine and dine in his house. They ate, drank, laughed and roared like lions. A behavior dated during pre-historical times as a fun way of making their presence known or as a way of showing their mighty dominion; thus, this, on the other hand, signals fear to any sort of rivals best unknown.

As we all know, it is in the nature of lions to roar in their territory; the same goes for giants. They are men and women who can mimicry roar, and it echoes as far as miles. Physical strength possessed in them often drives them to do what seems like the impossible. As soon as it was twilight, they all left for their respective homes with a gallon of take-home wine, each, as suggested by the Queen, for their families and friends.

13

THE NECKLACE

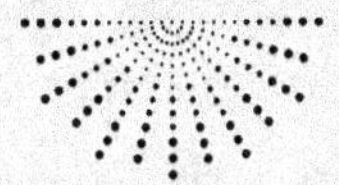

A new day came as usual, but something very odd and unheard of was observed. It is said that a mysterious catastrophe had mentally zombified the King, his undefeated forces who had wined and dined with him the previous day and an average of fourteen family members of each of the sixty warriors in the form of an active hangover from the excessive wine intake they had supposed.

One must understand that the giant tribe believes so much in warfare and strength. Therefore, each of the sixty combatant forces grows an average of fourteen family members, including their spouse, children, parents, grandparents, etc., aimed at withstanding any rival groups within and external. Therefore, an alarming number of eight hundred forty people were also mentally drained in just one night.

We also learned that those who were affected were those who drank the locally made sweet wine. We also learned that the gravity of their mental instability depends on the quantity one consumes, thus giving different body reactions or actions. Some were thrown into voiceless laughter; some were thrown into heavy sleep as though they were almost lifeless, while some were inactively awake, gushing unstoppable saliva.

A group of villagers who came to report their observation to their monstrous king but instead met the queen was also served the leftover sweet wine, with her assurance that the odd occurrence was a mere hangover of yesterday's merriment. The queen after that reached down to the empty wine tank, picked up her necklace, stared at it and wore it back around her neck.

Interestingly, we learn that the queen's necklace was responsible for the mental destruction that struck over eight hundred people. History has it that the moment she knew about the traditional house party with respect to the celebration of her newborn baby, she quickly dropped her poisonous necklace inside the wine tank. This necklace was given to her by the dwarf royal household for that very catastrophic purpose. She was said to have consulted the dwarf royal household while she was with them on just how to kill and conquer the ruler of the giant tribe without incurring any severe consequences to herself.

It was a poison, primitively designed and worn as a necklace, with its antidote worn on the left arm, made from the most toxic biological substances unknown that can destroy an entire human race. It is best to say that the dwarves, amongst a thousand other bad things, knew how to prepare a poison that could be instantly fatal to whosoever it might as little as touch with his lips. This means that an amount the size of a pin drop will kill a person as fat as anything.

"All tribes are dangerous, and no tribe is without dangerous people: the danger alone keeps a place at peace and not dangerous." Ultimately, we are surrounded by potentially dangerous people - it's the action that makes a person or people outwardly deadly.

This brings me to a philosophy that says: "All tribes are dangerous, and no tribe is without dangerous people: the danger alone keeps a place at peace or war." Ultimately, we are surrounded by potentially dangerous people – it is the action that makes a person or people outwardly deadly.

Unfortunately for the queen of Kruma, having waited several months for the best opportunity like that, the poisonous necklace lost most of its instantaneous and deadliest vice. Thus, the poison's result was different rather than massive death as expected.

Having eloped with as many treasures as she could lay her hands on, conveyed by two donkeys, she knew her death was imminent if she returned either to her tribe or the dwarf community. Any of these two tribes may want to kill her for either extreme hatred caused by the invasion of the giant tribe or greed for those treasures; therefore, she chooses to find a cave miles away from her clan and hide the treasures until she comes up with a good idea that will lead her home safely.

14

THE ARROWS OF ANGER

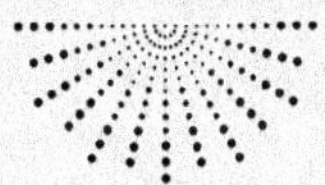

She thought of a pitiful scenery that would grant her entry into her kingdom; therefore, she tore her garment, separated the two donkeys, and killed and showered with the blood of one. She then returned to her community in a pool of blood, shouting and calling the attention of all her tribe's men, saying:

Where are my people!
Where are my men!
I have fought for seasons!
I have single-handedly defeated our invaders and enemies!
Come, my people, for it's time to go and take back our stolen treasures!

Her voice echoed across her clan as she was moving on her donkey towards her palace gently. Her strategy was perfect since no one attacked her. Of course, it was heart-melting seeing her in a pool of blood. Less they knew it was the blood of one of her donkeys. Not quite long after, her people gathered some primitive round-looking mats where hand-crafted weapons, especially spares and arrows, were preserved. It takes proper care to handle those arrows, considering the degree of poison they are made of, particularly in each of the pointed ends.

As soon as they got hold of their spears and arrows, she confidently led them to the giant tribe. And like an intense hurricane, they stormed the giant tribe in their thousands, including men and women, young and old; their men massacred and burnt all forms of mud castles that dwelled within its clan, as their women and children looted not just treasures but also hundreds and thousands of farm steeds and domesticated animals simultaneously in extremity. Their actions were unheard of in the history of Kruma and the entire Africa. It was really a load down of age-long nurtured griev-ances, forcing them to repeat the dreadful inva-sion over time without end.

Over the years, all these tribes have conceived an endless fascination for competitive war and balance of powers alike. Each misdeed received a tenfold penalty, with rewards of good deeds also proportional. Their challenge brings out the ugliest character in all participants and creates a severe and lasting past among those who fought. Thus, its mastery was a long, decisive pursuit. It was so easy to conquer the giant tribe as most of its powerful forces were in a vegetative state caused by the queen's poisonous necklace. The attack was one of the most cruel and sinister misdeeds that was ever committed, which left mutilated bodies at the mercy of scavenging vultures.

As if that was not enough, they stormed the giant tribe again. Still, this time, their purpose was to castrate the male teenagers as they could capture aimed towards slowing down their fertility rate since their significant giant stature was becoming alarming, hence leading to the destruction of an age. Anesthesia was not a thing of consideration during this horrendous process. Hot ashes and coals were used to cauterize the open wounds and massive bleeding. The fertility rate hence dropped.

The entire plot portrayed the gravity of a perfect love scam from a character I refer to as an angelic enemy (The Queen's character). However, seeing the mighty crushed, one of the Kruma's men joyfully said:

At the peak of Kruma's invasion into the giant tribe, the queen ensured no harm befall her baby and his keepers, who mainly were too humble and foolish older women, so that he may live to learn justly in the path of goodness and truth for he will in the future mount the throne of his monstrous-father, his crown and scepter, which ought to be his own by right of inheritance having known that the passage of mantles or properties from father to sons through several lineages among families are well known and unquestionable regardless of birth circumstance. Only at that point, she believe that both kingdoms will know peace and mutual co-existence.

Their outnumbering system of invasion was described as a human swarm. They also set free the baby-making captives. After that, the queen became the centerpiece of Kruma's military strength as she played a leading role in defeating their enemies. From the satisfactory reactions on their faces, one can tell how good it feels trampling on your enemies, especially when you are confidently sure you can defeat them. It feels like being on top of the world. However, apart from the poisonous aid given to her by the dwarves, it's hard to say if there was any other tribe that consorted with the Kruma people in the revenge mission.

Kruma continued to threaten that they would make life so miserable not just for the giant tribe but particularly for any suspected spy and their monstrous King who was mentally and physically motionless by the poisonous necklace too. During this invasion, the Kruma people purposely abducted the king of the giant tribe as their hostage in his motionless state. They were kept under the torture of dreadful witches in a place best referred to as the 'dungeon' on the outskirts of Kruma, where unmarried dead victims of war are also laid to rest, and it was rumored to house deep spiritual presence.

This dungeon is noted to be held firmly by a gang of 21 old witches whose dominion were tormented and whose dark magic has defiled the science of childbearing, owning to the fact they still give birth even in their old age. They were mothers of an average of 24 to 27 children each, most of which were eaten by these witches during their popular ritual of "blood and fire," especially those considered as having sweet blood while those of their children who are regarded as having bitter blood survived their torture; a culture of expulsion on the evolution of magic.

They were the most prolific single mothers in history, living under temporal tents scattered around the dungeon in such a dirty swamp. Although they outlived most of their children, they saw a few of them hold mantles in some shrines.

This portion of Kruma is significantly inhabited by a gang of witches who are known for wearing their evilness on their bodies and the nails of their fingers, and everyone else who is diabolically dreadful and dirty. Their dining concept is more or less a communion of vultures, squabbles and temporal jealousy. History has it that their ancestors were not wholly mortals. It also didn't tell us the length of time they lived, but we were told they engaged in so many spiritual invigorations that were unworthy of discussion.

There at the dungeon, they stripped off his regalia, turned his eyes heavenwards and suspended him with unbreakable chains against a huge lifeless tree trunk aimed until eternity for his intense inhumanity, self-aggrandizing craftiness and overwhelming covetousness. Even at death, he was still bonded with chains.

With those irremovable chains, he will never stand a chance of reincarnation, they believe. If he is granted a proper burial, he will possibly reincarnate, and of course, Kruma will obviously breathe fire from his next life's ruts. A ritual shrine is also noted at the edge of the dungeon where those witches cast into the spirits of the dead for two reasons: as a gateway to eternal rest or eternal hell. Without a doubt, he deserves eternal hell.

The villagers who often visit the site controversially ascribed that they have witnessed strange echoes of the enchantment of the unknown over the monstrous king and even encounter ghosts at odd hours, which they said are of his dead victims whose souls found joy over his eternal punishment. At dead night, the only souls that stick around are the souls of his victims and the witches, hovering and haunting the dungeon.

So successful as it sounds, the Queen has perfectly displayed her cleverness by captivating the undefeated without him realizing it, which, in the end, defines the ruler's accumulated wealth as a lifetime of useless efforts and unending frustration, especially looking at his bond with those chains. Onlookers and his limbless victims, who were still nursing the fury of his misdeeds, cut off his ears, cut open some parts of his body, left him earless and sat back as they watched him bleeding onto his naked body.

To some others, the punishment was insignificant because it was as though one is punishing the dead, for he has zero sense of stimuli at that point- that is to say that the punishment would have been best inflicted on him if he was himself and probably to choose where and how he will absorb his eternal punishment.

Although the queen was emotionally affected for a moment, having heard the susurrus sound made by his breath and watching the witch pets (the vultures) stand on either side of him, picking so deep into his blood-sac, she continued to watch the man she had lengthy intimacy with suffered through the perpetual bond to death. But for the benefit of peace and their safety, she allowed him to bear the consequences of his lifetime actions.

Right there, as the queen stood still gazing at him, she was quoted as saying before a massive gathering of onlookers, "Nothing idolizes the mind than when one is addicted to committing evil. For someone like him (the monstrous king) who can give up his sleep at dead night to nowhere, I can't imagine it is a thing of fear. However, he had gone out at dead night when he noticed a flash as exact as a digital camera. At first, he thought it could be lightning since he didn't know where precisely the flash came from, but when it happened the second time, he stopped and paid more attention as his eyes clocked around him.

Not quite long after, the supposed camera flashed again right from the bare ground before him. Then, he began to wonder for a moment who must have dropped such an object deliberately or involuntarily on his path. Due to poor illumination, he gently drew closer and bent down to view the object in question when a black cat-like creature dashed off from that spot.

It wasn't an object, as he thought after all. Having thought of what he saw, he knew a territorial demon was within his clan. Notwithstanding, he quickly dropped the notion because he had never believed in the existence of God, gods, demons, or any sort of principality all his life and wouldn't suddenly acknowledge such a thing at that point in his life.

In fact, he is known for saying, "Gods show your face if you exist!" especially when he has smoked their usual local herbs and drank out of limit. This, on the other hand, became a statement of jokes and greeting among him and his friends who, when they ran into each other, would smile and shout, "Gods show your face if you exist!" and to think of the fact that his philosophy changed the perception of those around him towards the existence of God and evil is disheartening.

I was unaware of his encounter until he had a dream about the same cat-like creature that accosted him that very night, the queen continued.

In his dream, he said, he was suddenly enveloped by the same black cat-like creatures with great force in that same spot as his life encounter. He said they were in thousands sucking, chewing and ravaging through his flesh. Although he fought relentlessly to shed the creatures off his body yet, they subdued him eventually. He was breathing so fast in what I supposed was his last breath, having been left to die in his pool of blood by those creatures, when I tapped at him, and he realized it was a dream. He stood up in shock and carefully ran his eyes all over his body before me, and not even a scratch was found by him.

He sat down quietly and began to ponder the nightmare. Thinking that his positive mind still told him that evil was eminent in his sphere of affluence is becoming a concern to him. His frantic countenances drew me closer, and I questioned him gently as he revealed his encounters.

Upon hearing this new turn of encounter from him, the queen immediately knew right inside her mind that the impeccable gods of the dwarves were imminent. Objectively beautiful as the queen was Mendaciousness and was effortlessly more charming before him. Thus, she was able to sway him away from any negative feelings he may have developed by reassuring him that no one, to their specific knowledge, would intend to bewitch him to death and get possession of his royal crown. She dismissed his thoughts as being impracticable with a resounding assurance. Her self-styled optimism was tinged with realism.

To the queen, she knew that if his negative feelings should grow out of bound, his people may likely persuade him to consult the man everyone knows, who dwelled at the foot of a lofty mountain and was reckoned a sage man, a soothsayer and a necromancer; who will perhaps foresee the danger (queen's plot) that lies ahead of him and his entire clan.

Going back to what I was told about the soothsayer, he has the power to conjure demons. He was also rumored to be making potions with the deadliest roots and participating in lustful associations with an unknown set of entities in human shapes.

It was not a thing of surprise that the monstrous king fell for the queen's antics because people like him are so addicted to the virtual world of beauty pursuit that they merely believe that anyone else's idea exists other than the desirable and ideal womanly icon before him. Not up to a week after the nightmare, the queen of Kruma and her troops revolted against him with the help of the poisonous necklace. Indeed, those cat-like creatures that ravaged through his skin were Kruma warriors in actual reality. Swiftly, they enveloped him like those living creatures he saw."

Going back to the cave where she had earlier killed a donkey and hid the first treasure she got from the giant tribe, she was baffled to discover from a little distance away that certain neck-impaired humans were feasting on the dead donkey and had equally claimed ownership of her treasures.

This unique cave and its surroundings are said to be inhabited by the most legendary neck-deformed humans and everyone else who is beautiful, violent and completely abnormal. They are also a clan of people known for wearing their burdens on their necks. History has it that their ancestors were humans/apes, although it didn't tell us how they came about or the length of time they lived. Still, we were told their existence is attributed to an imprecise evolution and changes worthy and unworthy of discussion. In this tiny tribe, one's safety can't be determined.

They are the minute number of human races she never knew existed, let alone had a home inside the cave. She was somewhat amazed by what she was seeing and angry over her lost treasures. One may ascribe their impaired necks to their constant head tilt under the cave, considering its compressing height, or rather a trait caused by fatal heredity.

By this surprise, she drew closer a little to spy on those neck-impaired humans and their lifestyle was nothing more or less of commotion like the howling of wolves or, instead, an outburst of profanity. One significant observation made by the queen of Kruma is that there is no culture of sexual boundary amongst them as a bunch of males take turns on every single female in a matter of minutes repeatedly, and from their satisfactory reactions, it is not unusual; a culture of continuous chaos and confusion.

They tend not to have the power of vocal sounds due to their impaired or compressed neck condition; thus, their reactions or behaviors are not clearly understood by an average person. One may be correct to say this is why they were unable to fit in among ancient civilized communities of ordinary people. They were utterly behind in developing any cultural lifestyle, not even the least of economic activity like farming. In fact, one would not be wrong to say that they are masters of nothing. People who have encountered their beauty look at some point in the forest and refer to them as devil's angels.

From the hardened wrinkles on their faces, they have probably stayed there for over ten decades. Suspiciously, they must be masters in the art of magic, considering the fact that there is no atom of a trace of farm workaround that sustains their lives or a trace of territorial ownership by a clan of responsible people. Further discovery shows that men and women are cultured in harvesting dead animal bones and making hand tools.

These hand tools and weapons helped them dig farther or maximize the space in the cave. They took digging as their hobby, and this enabled the minute tribe to continually create new empty chambers as their population increased. They continued to dig until their fingers were severely disfigured. Those twisted and bent fingers rank the bearers as lords of the cave. Such men are highly cherished for their selfless services in their lifetime.

Also, looking at the dirtiness of their skin, they don't seem to have taken their bath for as long as they have lived. She mumbled a few thanks to the gods that the occupants of the cave (neck-impaired humans) were outside the cave at the time of her arrival, and thus, she was able to see them first and not fall prey in their hands if not her intrusion would have turned out tragically.

She considers them unworthy opponents. Thus, a battle will be a waste, although she hopes to get hold of a calm and swift idea someday that will let her take back those treasures without a struggle, as they seem to have more lives than cats.

Unfortunately, this minute race could not survive the fate of time as the cave was said to have collapsed, resulting in massive death. Massive perforation and digging over time were attributed to the cause of the collapse. Henceforth, such races went into extinction.

She was famed as a warrior queen, the strongest and craftiest of all queens, who single-handedly plotted the defeat of the giant tribe and returned as many stolen treasures as possible—not just the treasures stolen from her kingdom alone but also treasures stolen from many other tribes the giants also had at some point invaded, therefore making her lineage and tribe overwhelmingly wealthier than ever before.

The literature of these tribes brings one to what I refer to as humanity's vain struggle in the pursuit of illicit intentions. I have discovered the dynamics of conflicts and warfare not just in Kruma but all around the world, which end each historical age and restart a new cycle continuously for an unending reason.

Everything, especially the victory over their defeat, was an unforgettable remark that marked the start of their life's most memorable moments, which was collectively agreed to be celebrated annually. Such a tradition of excellence comes not just from celebrating the great past of warfare but also from leading the people into the future. This victory hence extended beyond its dramatic form in Kruma. It influenced large portions of the greater region's tradition through the trend of war acrobatic dance, a dance of anger that demonstrates the defeated, thus retaining a special place of prominence within the new century for having survived the ravages of time.

Such war acrobatic dance, in the actual sense, portrays each of us in a frantic race against difficulties, hoping to fight off our fear someday. The energy during this annual celebration is eternally profound, and one can't quit listening or participating. It obsesses oneself and also leads the listener to the darkest corners of one's mind, blurring the lines between internal happiness and banked grievances.

While in Kruma, the queen hatched a plan to deploy and pay some able, trusted men from her clan to guide her newly born heir apparent to the giant throne to ensure no harm of any kind caused by any plot of hatred caused by her led invasion may befall the child. However, they were not informed that the child was hers.

Although she fears visiting the treacherous tribe, she finds many disguised ways to meet and declare motherly love to her newborn baby with lots of gifts for his welfare as well. Through the use of spies, as she learned, she gained partial control over the giant tribe.

As I usually tell my friends, the circumstance, which acts as a watchdog over humanity, has made what seemed to be the most significant achievement of the giant tribe an absolute failure while the tribes they referred to as cowards are setting up economic empires through the plot of their presumed weakness. Henceforth, the Kruma people achieved a sound foundation of tribal tolerance against acts that promote tribal hate and intolerance, therefore bringing safety to the people regardless of their origin, beliefs or race.

Today, her character has emerged as a significant inspiration for her literary and poetic significance, as a symbol and archetype to inspire new generations of poets and novelists. The three major tribes (Kruma, the giant tribe and the dwarf community) were indeed regions with abundant history and multicultural convergence.

THE WITNESS'S POEM

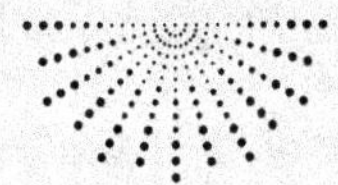

I'm the eyes that witnessed the horror
of the event's timeline
I'm the voice that spoke through
the age
I'm the conjured dreams in the minds
of princes but soon I discovered I'm
the centre of controversy

I'm the love that shines light on
our path
I'm the centre piece of admiration in
the world of man in this era
I'm the mouth that spoke brutal truth
through the age

When I met the horror of humanity in
the event of the tribal chaos, my body
suddenly became the racing mind

When I encountered the waves of
misdeed and the uncertainty of
vengeance my ears could hear the
unknown chanters in the void.

In the sphere of the entire plot lies
the shadows and mysticism of nature
I'm the art of history that revealed
the nemesis of errors against sinful
tribe

I followed the history of all the events
tailored down to the end yet no one
knows my name

I'm the war horse that ran through
the battle field yet none of the spears
and arrows pierced me

I'm the eyes that saw the episodes of
massacre in the era of balance of
power and defeat yet I didn't shed
tears

In the midst of dead bodies left at
the mercy of scavenging vultures, I'm
the only soul alive in the scene of
massacre

I'm the nemesis that continually made

the evil and the sinners cry eternally;
yet I'm hoping to be free someday
from the destructions of love

My mind wants to sleep a night
without the memories of those misdeed,
warfare and chaos since it's reflection
drowns my mind.

Unchain me from the darkness of these
war horrors and let my mind free
from the dreams that fail to make me
happy before it rips off my heart to
pieces and destroys me.

Ooh! love chase, you have chased and
pushed me off your door and buried
me deep into a space of confusion and
continued to hurt me till this day.

THE END

Facebook: KO Nwankwo

Whatsapp: +97471690048

Email: setplet@yahoo.com